No Grey Areas

By
Joseph N. Gagliano

Printed in the United States

ISBN: 978-0-9971248-1-1
E-ISBN: 978-0-9971248-0-4
Rebel Publishing
Rebel-Publishing@outlook.com
3104 E. Camelback #605
Phoenix, AZ 85016

Website
NoGreyAreas.com

Thoughts & Thanks

My Wife - What a journey…!

My Kids - I count my blessings each day for having each of you in my life. I couldn't have dreamt of having better kids. I hope you guys know how much you're loved…

Andre - You define the word "unconditional". Even though I have some years on you, I look to you as an example of the man I need to be.
You have effected and changed so many lives. Add mine to that list…

Mikey Cash - I will tell you till my dying day, you may never fully understand how you saved me…

Ryan - You're my little Brother. A true trusted friend. Not many days passed during my "darkness" that I didn't hear from you. You kept me filled with hope…

Dad - Things were never supposed to be this hard. You may not think I noticed or listened to things over the years, but know I did. I just messed them up internally. You will always be my hero…

To the ones I've hurt - All I can do is ask for your forgiveness. And, say that I'm still a work in progress…

To the haters - Little can be said. Except that we are ALL flawed in our own ways…

Contents:

Foreword   By Andre Wadsworth
   -3rd overall pick in the '98 NFL draft& Founder of Impact Church . . . . . . **ix**

Introduction. . . . .**xi**

Chapter One   Easy Money. **1**

Chapter Two   The 900 cash machine. **7**

Chapter Three   My early years **13**

Chapter Four   Gambling made easy. **25**

Chapter Five   The art of the "F – I – X". **29**

Chapter Six   The first game. **35**

Chapter Seven   The perfect weekend. **49**

Chapter Eight   Playing motivated **61**

Chapter Nine   Game three. **67**

Chapter Ten   Game four – The explosion **71**

Chapter Eleven   Investigated **83**

Chapter Twelve   Building Shammy Man **95**

Chapter Thirteen   Riding High **105**

Chapter Fourteen   Partners with the Devil **111**

Chapter Fifteen   Building up again – The world falls apart . . **125**

Chapter Sixteen   Investigated – Again **129**

Chapter Seventeen $90 bill at Chili's **137**

Chapter Eighteen   Attorneys are born liars **143**

Chapter Nineteen   The Pain Within. **149**

Chapter Twenty   The Pit of Darkness **155**

Chapter Twenty-One   Right Place at the Right Time. **161**

Chapter Twenty-Two   9 months to get it all back. **169**

Chapter Twenty-Three   Sentenced... Again **181**

Chapter Twenty-Four   A Little Happiness... Before the Storm. . . **185**

Chapter Twenty-Five   Prison, the Second Time Around **193**

Chapter Twenty-Six   The Rear View Mirror **201**

About the Author **207**

Foreword

By:
Andre Wadsworth
1998 NFL 3rd Overall Pick & Founder of Impact Church

——————— ═══════ ═══════ ———————

This book *"No Grey Areas"* introduces you to a man and his choices (past, present and *"future"*). Choices he made that continually kept molding him into the person we all strive to be: a giving friend, a caring spouse and a loving parent.

Whether we want to recognize this or not, in some form or fashion we all want to be a GOOD LEADER and WINNERS in this so called "GAME" of life. Though leadership may be hard to define, the one characteristic common in all leaders is their ability to "MAKE THINGS HAPPEN" and Joe definitely has that talent.

This book holds true to the saying that the two most important things embraced by others in life are "RELATIONSHIPS" and "MONEY." That said because they're always the closest things to you!

I remember my dad telling me "Regardless of what came BEFORE or what has yet to come   what matters MOST RIGHT NOW is how YOU choose to respond to the CIRCUMSTANCES in front of you!"

The key word is "CHOOSE" and the CHOICE is yours to make…. good or bad!

Throughout the book you will see Joe Gagliano aka "Joey" (that's what I like to call him), make choices that will have you saying WOW, this guy must like pain. He made some foolish early life choices that led him down a path to rationalize the acceptance of "grey areas." Each choice made only with hopes to overcome a prior mistake.

Joe makes no excuses in the process of writing this because he openly acknowledges having all the opportunities one could wish for. Yet, along the way, he drifted. He drifted and then had to pay a price for the bad choices made.

Joe actually owns up to all choices made, and admits without shame, to being one of the stupidest "smart" guys you will ever meet. That growth process was learned through a painful life journey. One that is detailed in this story. Starting all the way back with a few early life defining moments.

Pain teaches us all lessons. But, pride seems to keep us from learning those lessons.

Chapter after chapter you'll witness the transformation of his youthful pride and ego into a man of clear purpose, conviction and humility. I believe that transformation only took place, because after all the suffering endured, he finally decided to "CHOOSE" the right people, surroundings and thoughts. The rest of the process fell into place from there.

"Watch your thoughts, for they become words. Watch your words, for they become actions. Watch your actions, for they become habits. Watch your habits, for they become character. Watch your character, for it becomes your destiny."

Andre Wadsworth

Introduction

The buzzer sounded. I had just fixed *three* college basketball games in a row, and I gently smiled as a cool *five* million dollars went right into my pocket. A few short years later, however, my joy and abundance would come to an end…almost to the point of suicide. As of this writing, I'm sitting on a wooden stool, typing my story on an antiquated twenty-plus-year-old typewriter, with no correction tape, while currently an inmate in a federal prison for the 2nd time in my life.

Who am I? Why should you care?

I'm a guy who has made poor choices for the sake of greed and success. A guy who applied God-given talents to build wealth and success, and then managed to misapply those talents and got a very different end result. A guy who charted a path that took him into grey areas and then had to pay the price for those ill-fated choices.

I am the guy with a story that can make a difference…a real difference in your life or the life of someone you know.

Bad results did not happen to me overnight, but rather through a series of poor choices and decisions that ultimately resulted in my downfall. I am a guy who is here to shine a bright light on the very painful, dark and public journey that I've endured so that I might positively impact others.

You may not be wandering into that grey area of your life right now. But, at some point in every person's life, temptation is placed before you. What you do with that choice is up to you.

I chose poorly.

This story is about the trading markets, a national sports scandal, building successful companies, losing everything (a few times), pursuing love, fighting suicidal depression, and finding redemption through faith.

My roller coaster ride stems from a single, early and fateful life choice I made in 1993. Remember the Arizona State men's basketball point shaving scandal? The one in which four college games were fixed?

That was me.

I organized and financed the entire scandal when I was a naive twenty-four-year-old, and to this day it remains one of the largest scandals in sports history.

I have never spoken about it, and I never wanted to. Over the years I have turned down many lucrative offers because I did not want to tell my story for the sake of entertainment or to turn a quick buck. I always knew that if I told the story, it had to serve a positive purpose for others.

I never had interest in a spotlight, or to put my family through that dark journey once again. But now, after having to accept a plea bargain on a second felony solely because I was an "easy" target,

I have both a story *and* lessons that need to be shared.

By telling my story, I'm willing to painfully expose my life's journeys with hopes of affecting others, to influence others, to warn others, and to share life lessons others may benefit from.

I am not here to make excuses, play the role of a victim, or shift the blame away from my due. If anything, I'm here to admit that I'm probably about the stupidest "smart" guy you will ever meet. Despite having just about every opportunity that life can offer, I chose to embrace the dark side of greed and relish material excess from impressionable moments imbedded in me at a young age, and even stronger impressions learned from the "legitimate" business world.

My story will take you from the elation of million dollar moments to the shame of telling your kids you are on your way to prison. This journey also goes into a dark depression only few survive. Depression so deep, that it had me searching for the "Top 10 ways to kill yourself" after I pled guilty and officially became a *two-time* felon.

Regrets? My biggest regret is not the loss of millions of dollars nor my possessions, nor even going to prison. What I regret most was the wasted time. Wasted, because of time I could have spent being a better father, a better person, a better friend, a better husband. Wasted, because I know I could have used my talents in many other ways to do amazing things, to make a difference in the world.

This is NOT a story of love,

But it is a loving one…

This is NOT a story of scandal,

But there were a few…

This is NOT a story of greed and corruption,

But it contains plenty…

This *IS* a story that finally gives the *true* details on one of the largest sport scandals in U.S history. The ASU point shaving episode is only a small part of my personal journey. My story describes life choices I made and how I sped down a dangerous path.

I hope you will find this story inspiring and motivating enough to give you a new perspective on how little, seemingly minor decisions, can lead you down a one-way street of financial, moral, and spiritual suicide.

No rational person begins life with dreams of cheating their way to the top. Or that this green stuff we call money is the end-all be-all of everything. And yet… sometimes it happens; one thing leads to another and before you know it, you're not who you thought you'd be… a person you would never have recognized in your early years.

You may have planned for success…

You may have planned to change the world…

But decades later you end up at ground-zero of one of the biggest sports scandals in the history of this country, and find yourself hit with *two* Federal prison terms.

Certainly not what my six-year-old self would have imagined.

I blame no one but myself for what happened; no one was holding a gun to my head saying, "Get rich at any cost or else." I made the choices, they were wrong, I got caught, and had to pay the price… with interest. That, I freely admit. But now it's time to make up for that wasted time and, with God's help, help others stay on the straight and narrow path.

With that in mind, I want this book to serve as more than an accurate telling of the inner details of the ASU scandal, my personal events, or the details on the self-serving nature of the criminal justice system.

My hopes are that this book will serve as a reminder to anyone using the same excuses as I did when it comes to right or wrong, - a loud alarm to anyone who thinks he can operate in the grey areas and not lose control.

THERE ARE NO GREY AREAS.

Rather, consider this my entry for Career Day at your school; my way of saying, "Hey kids, here's what *not* to do and what to look out for." A road map, if you will, of the types of hazards to expect if you lose your way, with insight along the way into what happened behind the scenes.

Greed is a cancer, a trap. It will blind you, blur your vision, and twist your perspective of the priorities in life to the point that it will cause you to lose and risk far more than you bargained for. It begins with a small, single step. It may be the one choice you make in life that seems innocent enough at first. You may not even know that fateful step when you take it. But that step, no matter how small you may think it is, will have a consequence in the future.

That first step being just one degree off today will result in being miles away from your true self down the road.

This is the story that starts with my first steps and the complicated dark path it led me on. My sincere hope for this story - my story - is to influence your thinking as you take your own steps.

May you make far better decisions than I did.

Chapter One:

Easy Money

"The Wolf of Wall Street" had it all wrong. Money is not the most seductive drug in the world…"

Easy money is.

It was on the trading floor of the Chicago Board of Trade, at the age of twenty-three, where for the first time in my life I knowingly compromised my integrity for the lure of easy money. Before I started at the CBOT, I was at a family party a few months earlier where I was introduced to a relatively successful bond futures trader by the name of Tony Stack. Tony was in his mid-fifties, an Italian guy who simply oozed money. He had a flair for the good life and loved to show off his successes in any way he could. Several drinks into our talk Tony asked me if I wanted to work for him as a clerk on the floor of the CBOT. At that time, I had no idea what a trading clerk was or what he did, but I did know clerks worked in the financial markets, and that was enough for me. I said "Yes" before my drink hit the table. I dropped out of college that same week, and went to work.

I loved everything about the financial markets from the very first day. The pace, the lifestyle, and the flash were all intoxicating. But most of all I was drawn to the nonstop action. I came to learn that a true trader has a mindset that defines the words "long term" as not exceeding five minutes. It was an instant gratification lifestyle, one that only cemented my, "I want it now" way of thinking.

The trading floor, or the "pit", of the CBOT is the pumping heart of the bond trading universe. In this Chicago landmark, I witnessed the ease and speed in which millions of dollars would change hands in the blink of an eye. The trading floor was choreographed chaos on steroids, run by hordes of sweaty traders wearing different styles and colors of jackets so they wouldn't all look the same, each one spitting and yelling their buy/sell orders to others while using hand gestures that bordered on obscene.

While there is an appearance of rivalry from the outside looking in, I can tell you that is not the case at all. Sure, there were daily fights that broke out as jacked up alpha males fought for their space and power, but we all knew we were part of a small, rather exclusive club. So, the disagreements rarely got personal. We traded while jammed like sardines into what looked like a modern day UFC octagon. While the trading was going on in the pits, the clerks circled; trying to keep an accurate running account of their traders' market positions.

The bond futures market Tony traded was one of the most expensive financial markets to trade. There was money, and tons of it, on that trading floor. The floor was broken up into two groups. First, you had the "Traders." Traders were made up of two kinds of people: ones that traded their own accounts and money, versus the ones who filled orders for others like banks or retail business. "Clerks and Runners" comprised the second group. These guys worked for the traders in an admin type of role, keeping their traders organized and manning the phones for incoming orders.

It didn't take me long to learn the ropes on the floor, or to figure out that the market was nothing more than a giant, legal casino. Sure, there's the argument that there is an art to understanding the market and having a feel for its direction, but I boiled it down to the basics. And, just like any casino, there always has to be a winner and a loser every time.

As a clerk for Tony, I would keep his trading house organized, work the phones, take orders, and arbitrage those orders into the trading pits. I was learning this world at an accelerated pace, and it came easily to me. In fact, from the very first day, the CBOT fit me like a glove. There was only one thing missing.

I didn't have a vice.

Curiously, all successful traders did. It was pretty safe to say that the bulk of the people in that financial world, or on the trading floor, either had drug or gambling problems. Personally, I'd never tried a drug in my entire life, but while at the CBOT I can assure you that I certainly learned to gamble.

The grouping of phones I manned for Tony had me crammed shoulder-to-shoulder next to a retail brokerage group and some of their employees. One of those employees was a guy named Rocco Lo-Freddie. We called him Rock. With a name like that, there was no way you'd confuse him with anything other than a tough street kid from Italian immigrants. His short black hair was shiny enough to be a distraction, but in the early 90's it was almost the norm.

The way Rock walked into a room was a dead giveaway that he'd grown up on the streets. He looked right into your eyes when he spoke to you, but every minute or so he'd glance around to the side or behind him so quickly you'd hardly notice. I'm not sure if this was from being raised in a tough neighborhood, or just a nervous tick.

But Rocco also had an infectious smile, laughed effortlessly, and always gave you a slap on the back when you left. He was a street kid trying to work his way up, aspiring to one day trade his own account in the pits just like me. He was extremely well liked on the floor, so hanging out with him got me into the "in crowd" pretty quickly.

Together, we had more in common than two Italians simply having vowels at the end of our last names. Our personalities were very similar when it came to the life, pace, and fast action of the CBOT. The noise, energy, and millions of dollars that moved between our fingertips was intoxicating to both of us.

As clerks, we were not earning anywhere near what the traders did, but we knew we were paying our dues and learning the industry. We learned the trade by watching our traders. There was simply no other way to earn your stripes in that world.

Rock was the first person I had met on the floor, or in my life up to that point, who actually enjoyed cutting corners and looked at all possible angles for short cuts. I'd never met a guy who took so much joy in trying to create that extra edge. It was with Rock, at the ripe age of 23, that I did the first truly unethical thing in my life.

I remember that day like it was yesterday. The trading floor was still noisy, but the pace had settled down enough for us to have a quick conversation. Rock walked up to me to talk…

"Hey, Joey," he barked.

"What's up?"

"Let's do a square for the Super Bowl. We can sell each square for a thousand bucks apiece."

"Sounds OK, Rock. But, that's a hundred thousand dollars."

If you're unfamiliar with a square, it's a grid with ten rows vertical, and ten rows horizontal. Each row gets a number assigned to it from 0 to 9. If the numbers you get in your square match the last digits for both teams at the end of each quarter or the final score, you win a percentage of the pot collected.

I ended up thinking that this would be a good way to meet and bond with a few of the higher profile traders.

But Rock had other plans for this square.

"Don't worry, Joey," he said. "We'll fix the thing."

"Man, what do you mean?"

"We'll sell half of the squares," he explained, "collect fifty thousand dollars from these guys, and for the other half of the squares we'll will put our own names in."

"Put our own names in? I'm not putting fifty thousand dollars into the pot! Are you crazy?" I said.

"No man, we'll make up a bunch of names, fill those names into fifty boxes, and assign the prime numbers where we need them to tilt the odds in our favor."

I remember drifting off while he was talking. Trying to unwind this concept of the legit way this should be done versus the scam Rocco was laying out to me. I broke it down in my mind. If we took the "prime numbers" in football like 0, 3, 4, 6, and 7 and assigned them to the fifty boxes we filled in, we pretty much controlled the board, and the odds went in our favor. The gambler inside me knew that greatly increased odds were all I needed. Rock was the devil on my shoulder saying things I knew better on.

I would like to say that I mulled this decision over and paused a while before saying yes to this scheme...

I would like to say that Rocco talked me into it...

I would like to say a lot of things...

Most of all, I would like to be able to recheck my moral compass and turn back the clock and said, "No thanks."

But I didn't...

The fast money and rapid decision-making had been imprinted on me for good. I knew that the choice I was making at that time was wrong, but rationalized it by thinking that it was still a gamble, and by convincing myself that those traders snorted, drank, and whored thousand dollar bills in their sleep.

To me, having them betting on a fixed game wasn't like robbing a bank or stealing from little old ladies. My moral compass was not absolute; I believed there was a grey area and this was it. My parents raised me to know better, but I continued to make excuses. Excuses that those guys would never miss a thousand dollars, and that it wouldn't affect their lives one bit. As a clerk, however, at the age of twenty-three, the concept of a fast fifty thousand dollars for Rock and me was amazingly seductive. Too seductive…

"Sure, let's do it." I instantly said.

The day of the game I was nervous. The gambler's itch was rushing adrenaline through my body as Rock and I watched the game together. We raked in all three quarters and the final score, splitting the fifty-thousand profit between us.

Looking back now, I honestly wish I had lost it all, or at least a large portion of the money on that scheme.

I wish that a safety would have been scored in the game to mess up the numbers, or that there had been a few missed extra points. Losing money that day might have almost scared me straight at that crucial point in my life. But it didn't happen that way; I won, and it was a quick twenty-five thousand of easy money in my pocket that no one asked questions about.

That decision and the speed at which I made it now rolls through my brain in slow motion. At the time, it happened in less than a second. Now, twenty plus years later, writing these words from inside a federal prison, I remember how quickly I spoke those fateful words…

"Sure, let's do it."

I wish now that someone would have slapped me silly for even thinking about it. The saying, "I wish I would know now what I didn't know then" really hits home.

The ripples of my actions began to gain momentum…

Chapter Two:

The 900 Cash Machine

With easy money in my pocket and me convincing myself that no one got "hurt" because of it, I wanted more. The NBA season was running full tilt, the baseball season about to launch, and I was ready to take advantage of it. During this era, 900 phone numbers were everywhere. If a phone call was made to a 900 number, there was no disputing that bill with the phone company; you either paid the bill in full or your phones got turned off.

It was the countless phone banks on the trading floor of the CBOT waiting to be milked that gave birth to my creation: Wizard Sports. I established Wizard to charge $24.95 per call to provide a nightly winning sports pick. My plan was not to advertise Wizard's 900 number or touting services. Instead, I wanted to use the countless CBOT's phones to make calls to Wizard's 900 line. Each call we made brought me almost $25 bucks. Every way I looked at this, it seemed like there was no risk. I knew that the traders and big house firms would never allow their phones, their lifelines to money, to be disconnected, and with the volume of calls on their lines, there was hardly a chance someone would detect the extra charges for my calls.

Rock was onboard before I could even finish explaining the plan, and we started making calls at every opportunity. The goal was to average fifty calls a day. That was an extra thousand plus a day in the pocket. Again, I knew it was wrong; I knew this wasn't what I was supposed to be doing with my life. But there was a Robin Hood aura to it; we were taking pocket change from millionaires and big companies. The part I ignored, of course, was that we were not giving it to the poor.

There were days when the markets were slow and I made hundreds of calls to Wizard's phone lines. Rock and I made as much making these calls as we did as clerks. This gravy train lasted for months. And, like all easy money, my "stealing from the rich" spilled over to victims who were not so deserving of my Robin-Hood pilfering.

Down the street from the CBOT, there was a couple that owned and operated a small Greek deli. I would go there almost daily to grab a bite. The owners were kind to me, always calling me by name, and letting me sit at the front counter to eat fast and watch the markets. A couple times a week I would ask to use their house phone. Who did I call?

Yep... Wizard Sports.

Pure greed, that's all it was. Greed had managed to twist and destroy my core values of right and wrong into a far deeper shade of grey. In fact, greed and easy money at that point had eliminated any shades of grey that were left, and just took me directly to a deep and utterly ugly black pit.

With some investments I made while in college kicking out monthly dollars, my actual job as a clerk with Tony paying me well, not to mention personally trading a few bonds myself, fixing the Super Bowl square, and scooping in the daily income from Wizard sports, I was doing pretty well at the young age of twenty-three. So much so that I ended up moving downtown to Lincoln Park and bought a new corvette to drive every now and again. I had plenty of cash on hand and my bank accounts were growing. What I didn't have was a social life, so I took a "job" so that I could get out more.

I was a fairly good looking kid - a "gym rat" in really good shape- and making more money than most twenty-three year olds. I never did any drugs or did the social BS bar scene, so when the job at the

Sugar Shack was offered to me, it sounded like it was the answer to my social needs.

The Sugar Shack was an upscale all-male strip club in Stone Park, IL. It mainly hosted bachelorette parties on Thursdays, Fridays, and Saturday's with two shows a night. I worked there as a waiter, wearing spandex shorts, no shirt, cuff links, and a bow tie. The waiters had their own dance skit for the shows, and I had more phone numbers on napkins shoved down my shorts on a nightly basis than I could possibly count. It was just a ton of fun for me, with a great group of guys, and a lot of good memories.

With tons of cash on hand, and after about a year on the trading floor, I started gambling... Mainly sports betting. I remember the first account I got with a bookmaker. It was certainly not hard to get because most of the runners on the trading floor were either drug dealers, gamblers, or bookmakers. If that was the type of business you were in, the CBOT was the perfect place for you to be.

Looking back at the start of my gambling career, I guess the worst thing that could have happened to me - or any other gambler - was to have success early on. Beginner's luck ends up translating into a curse. Winning without suffering losses creates a sense of infallibility. I suffered badly from this. I was now twenty-four years old, with sizable bank accounts, and a daily cash flow that rivaled that of some of the floor traders. But on top of this, I was on an *incredible* winning streak. *Way too much!* I was simply "on a tear" and could do no wrong; the art of sports betting consumed me. Searching for advantages in games and betting lines occupied most of my thoughts.

All of this was going on while my younger brother Nick was attending Arizona State University. Back in those days, my brother and I had a fairly decent relationship. He and his friends would call me "The Preacher" because I was always trying to keep them on the straight path and preach to them life lessons I learned in hopes of keeping them out of trouble.

I should have listened to my own words.

Every now and again I would make trips to Tempe to visit Nick and his friends. I remember those college kids as very impressionable. On those trips I always brought cash with me, and *lots* of it. When I was in Tempe, it was assured that Nicky and his friends would have a good time. It seemed like they looked up to me, and that they thought I was on the "right track" in life. So much so, that many of them would often just call me back in Chicago and ask for advice on random things.

Particularly, betting on sports.

Turns out that on one of my trips to Tempe, one of the guys my brother introduced me to was a kid named Benny Silman. Benny was a short, Jewish kid from New York who lived in the same building as Nicky, and while he was a student at ASU, he was also the ever-aspiring entrepreneurial bookmaker on campus.

Up to that point my life experiences while at the CBOT showed the lousy choices I willingly chose to make. I was not pressured into those poor decisions. I knowingly made them, and in some cases initiated them. Oddly enough, at that time in my life, I wrongly believed that I was living in a "normal" type of world. Of course, I know now that I was then smack dab in the center of a complete and unsustainable fantasy world. A world that praised ill-gotten power, rewarded fast wealth, and revered ruthless behavior.

That was what I learned while at the CBOT. I learned that saying someone was an honest – ethical trader is one of the bigger oxymorons in the world. The public simply has NO clue how the markets are manipulated and the fixed ways dollars change hands. Smart institutional money directs the markets. Traders know the news, details and vital facts needed long before any newspapers come close to the information.

I saw all that first hand. I was in the middle of the mad center of the financial universe where I was exposed to the culture of a trade; a cutthroat business with accepted tendencies to step over the line into the grey - and beyond. I'm not using my environment as an excuse, but being an impressionable twenty-three year old kid who was looking to fit in, my mindset was shaped by the actions around me.

Lesson: Choose your environment carefully.

Looking back at things, I realized that although a few of the things I referenced weren't exactly ethical, financial success came easy to me; maybe too easy. I knew I had a gift. A gift to be a visionary. To create concepts and see them through to completion. But, because of the markets, what I lacked was the respect for money that people who have a hard time earning it develop. Internally, for me, it seemed like success was expected. Not to say that I didn't feel I worked hard for what I had, but it seemed that being looked up to as a success or "big shot" by others was the drug I craved.

I wish I could turn back time to my youth.

Chapter Three:

My Early Years

I was just like a lot of six-year-olds in the northwest side of Chicago. Grew up in a quiet neighborhood, middleclass, with kids playing ball in the street… your typical home life. I was raised Italian Catholic, went to a Catholic grade-school and an all-boys Catholic High School, so two-color uniforms and God were daily presences in my life. I guess you could only call us Catholics in the technical sense, as we only went to church on the "big" days. You know what I mean - Christmas, Easter, the occasional wedding or funeral, and the rest of the time we pretty much paid lip-service to it all. After all, if God is everywhere then why do I have to go to church?

I was the middle of three kids, with an older sister and a younger brother, in a strong Italian-American family. Both of my parents' parents came straight from Sicily; my Mom was an only child and my Dad was one of *seven* children. There was no shortage of aunts to pinch my cheeks or cousins to run around with. We were one hundred percent Sicilian and proud of it. I believed I had all the extended family I'd ever need to reign me in if I got out of line.

Of course, it didn't seem to work out that way.

The naïve, Italian boy who grew up in the 70's bears little resemblance to the man I am today. As a young man, I was a slightly awkward and pretty introverted. It didn't help that I had to wear braces for seven years of my life. In those days the orthodontic headgear made me look like I was trying to tune in a radio station with my teeth. If that wasn't bad enough, my shyness came on strong into my early teens and the "Acne Years." At one point, my acne got so bad I thought of naming a couple of the craters on my face after ones on the moon.

I think the Sea of Tranquility started around my left cheekbone. Thankfully, though, by the time I was a junior in high school the acne, along with my shyness, had cleared up.

My dad was a bailiff for the Chicago-area courts. He became a Chicago Police officer for twelve years before starting his own security and private investigations firm when I was about eight or nine years old. With his character as my guide, it's not as though I was raised in a criminal environment—quite the opposite. And yet, even with a solid family life and a father in law enforcement, I still managed to somehow drift into the grey areas and allow my moral compass to be compromised when confronted with a "right" or "wrong" choice.

Those early days were pretty lean, though my parents never let on how bad it really was. For instance, hot dogs were served most nights to feed us all, but my Mom would make light of things by calling them "tube steaks." After all, my Dad was stretching a police officer's wages to feed and support *three* kids, and my Mom stayed at home to raise us all.

Once my Dad's security business started picking up, Mom was brought in to handle most of the administrative tasks and payroll for the company. During my freshman year of high school the company started doing well… very well, actually. My dad landed his first major account to provide security guard service for most of the True Value Hardware manufacturing plants in the Midwest, as well as their internal private investigations work.

Being just a flat out good man, and in law enforcement, my Dad was always viewed as a straight-shooter; an honest man respected by all. But, to be absolutely transparent, with a last name like Gagliano and a large Sicilian family, it's pretty fair to say that not everyone in our circle of family and friends was 100 percent pure. In fact, Dad would always make a point to warn me about certain relatives.

"Joey, don't hang out around them," he would say, "because when you ask them for a favor, they'll expect ten in return."

Unlike many other things he said that I should have listened to, that comment, in particular, did stick with me. Maybe if I'd listened to more of the other pearls of wisdom, I would have created a much different future.

As my Dad's success continued, both my parents developed a fondness for traveling and they both *loved* their trips to Las Vegas. Dad had a good friend who ran Bally's Hotel, so anytime my parents made a trip out there they were always treated well. It was one of their Las Vegas trips that made the biggest impression on me.

I was around eleven years old at the time. I was left back in Chicago with my brother and sister in the care of my aunt. My parents were supposed to be back home on that Sunday, but I remember my dad calling the house to say they were staying in Vegas a couple extra days. It's been more than thirty-five years since that call, but I still remember hearing his voice on the phone like it was yesterday. His tone was very steady, but when I asked him why he was staying those few extra days, his energy quickly took an uptick.

"Joey... Daddy's having a *really* good trip!"

But what did he mean? Was he having a particularly relaxing stay? Something good about the shows? What was so good about the trip? I had to know, so I asked.

"Joey, I'm winning a *lot* of money." He said...

That was the day I learned that Vegas is not a place for relaxation, or shows, but a place for MONEY. You went to Vegas to make *money* and make it *quick*. Fast money was the reason for his excitement. I was eleven, and his words and voice stuck with me, a lesson permanently imprinted on my brain.

When my parents finally got home and unpacked, my Dad put five large envelopes on the desk, each of them looking practically pregnant with hundred-dollar bills in them. Then he put one of the packets in my hand and let me open it. I was in shock! To my eleven-year-old mind, I was holding all the money in the world, and it belonged to my Dad. He was so proud of what he'd done, particularly in front of me, his oldest male child; he who would carry on his name. That look on his face stuck with me for life. Money was good, more money was great, and the faster and easier you could get it the better.

I wish I'd never seen that envelope.

There was another incident a few years later that further served to solidify my warped concept of money. It was during my sophomore year in high school. Dad rarely woke up early in the morning - he and I have that in common. Since he owned the company, he usually started his days around nine or ten in the morning with a cup of coffee, some pound cake, and the newspaper at the kitchen table. I still miss that vision.

A couple times of the year, though, True Value Hardware would have their big convention in downtown Chicago, and my dad and his company would be burning the midnight oil to make sure his clients were happy. His schedule would vary between getting up early to never having gone to bed in the first place. It was during one such convention that I was able to get a ride to school from him.

It was the perfect Kodak moment; the kind you see at the beginnings of a family movie just before things go horribly wrong. My dad had just bought a brand new baby blue Lincoln town car and treated it like his fourth child. On this particular day he was dressed up in a grey pinstripe suit and looking very GQ, and all because of the convention. I knew it had to be important, because about the only time my Dad wore a suit was on holidays, weddings, or funerals, and this wasn't any of those.

Usually, getting to school was similar to a Homer Greek epic. First there was the four-block trek to the nearest bus stop, which would take me to a train, then from the train onto another bus just to get to the main street that was still four blocks away from my school, then start hoofing it for that last leg, hoping I'd make it on time. Chicago winters were *real* fun with those journeys. The only thing missing was the abominable snowman.

Being fifteen and getting a ride from my Dad in the middle of a snow-bound Chicago winter, however, was the equivalent of seeing Santa Claus with the lost Ark of the Covenant on his sleigh; it was a *very* good thing. That particular day we didn't talk much on the way to school, but I did have a problem I needed to talk to him about. We were about ten minutes away from the drop off before I finally got the nerve to bring up my question. Keep in mind that I was a shy kid, covered in a face full of acne, with braces and a stutter. I think the conversation went something like this…

"Uh, Dad?"

"Yup?"

"I… Well, there's this dance."

"Your first high school dance? My boy's growing up."

"Yeah, well, it… It's going to be at the Resurrection High School for Girls."

Talking to him about girls was tough enough. The grin that was on his face didn't help much.

"Dad, *please.*"

"Okay, continue." He said…

"Well, there's the dance and I don't have… anything cool to wear."

"Any particular girl you're trying to impress?"

"Dad, you're not helping. I just, well, I need some help. I want to go to the dance but don't have anything to wear. So, I was wondering if, maybe…"

We had reached the school parking lot by this point, and I remember my Dad looking at me, putting the car in park, then leaning to one side so he could reach into his pocket. He pulled out a wad of cash that could literally have choked a horse. I just know my eyes went wide when he asked,

"How much do you need?"

"I don't know. I need to buy pants and a shirt… Maybe fifty bucks?" I said back…

And then, like a high roller handing over a tip for the lady with the tray of drinks, in such a cool way that I will never forget, he peeled off two hundred-dollar bills and said,

"Go have fun."

For a moment I was paralyzed with shock as those two bills dropped into my grasp.

"Thanks Dad! Wow!"

I nearly sprang out of the car and strutted across the parking lot. I had two *hundred* dollars on me. I was important. Who needs drugs? This is the sort of high that I want. From that day forward, money was my drug of choice. I had become a cash junkie.

After all the mistakes I've made since then, and, as you'll see, there have been a lot, I still return to those two defining moments as the start of my warped and misguided view of money. Views that I still struggle to shake, like any old addict. Don't get me wrong, both my mom and dad were savers, and constantly preached the importance of saving twenty to thirty percent of everything made. But I never listened. I always thought I knew a better way.

Anyone who really knows me will tell you that the actual money means very little to me. What I think happened is that somehow I led myself to believe that *if* I was able to place myself into the role of "Big Shot" then people would overlook my inadequacies, insecurities, my acne, the stuttering, and much later in life the felony conviction. Man, was that way of thinking ever wrong.

Because of my messed up sense of reality, school and I never saw eye to eye either. And yet somehow I managed to graduate high school. The problem was, my parents had visions of at least one of their kids getting a college degree. College was not something I was looking forward to, but lucky for me, the girl sitting in front of me during my college ACT entrance exam scored a 19 on her test.

Not so coincidentally, so did I. That 19 was the lowest possible score I needed to get into Eastern Illinois University without them looking too carefully at my two-point-nothing high school GPA.

EIU wasn't really a bad place, and it earned bonus points by being about three hours away from our home in Chicago; far enough to be alone but near enough if I ever needed family behind me.

I never really wanted to go to college, but my parents were both so proud when we first toured the EIU campus. Neither my mom nor my dad nor his six other siblings had ever gone to college, and both sets of my grandparents were fresh off the boat from Italy and uneducated. Imagine the pride, then, that I saw in their eyes as we walked onto that campus. I would be the first in the family to go to college, and since they could afford it… Well, I didn't want to let them down; it was important to them.

So I packed up the Pontiac Firebird they'd bought me and headed down to Charleston, Illinois to give college a try.

Not much of a try, I'll admit. I treated college as a joke from the moment I set foot on campus. I lived in a dorm my freshman year, signed up for a full load of classes, and even pledged a fraternity. Not that I attended most of my classes, but I at least signed up for them.

I remember my first class and the first time I was exposed to the college way of doing things. The small room with the little desks was gone, replaced by a lecture hall that looked like the Hollywood Bowl, with over two hundred students attending, all crowded in like sardines, and no one taking attendance. I was distracted. I wasn't listening or learning anything; the instructor could have been lecturing on the finer points of underwater basket weaving for all I knew.

It wasn't long, then, before I started getting the notes from other students, and focused my efforts on lining up people to sit next to during a test or quiz, or working angles to get a sick note from the campus clinic and arranging for a copy of the test to be copied down from others when I took the test later. Attempting to cheat my way through college was a *ton* of work, let me tell you.

More work, in fact, than the actual studying would have been. Looking back on those years, I always think that if I'd put as much effort into applying myself to my studies as I did into circumventing the system, then I would have been a real scholar, and not be in prison writing this for you.

As it was, in the two years that I attended EIU, I amassed maybe fifteen college credits with a GPA that couldn't even start a car on a cold Chicago morning.

So what *did* I spend all my time doing? I *did* say that I joined a fraternity. Pledging Sigma Pi constituted the bulk of my first semester in college. I remember telling my Dad that I was thinking of joining the "Greek life" on campus. He was so upset with me, telling me, "Joey, why aren't you joining the Italian clubs?" That still makes me laugh to this day.

It was during my second semester that the early impressions learned to be a "Big Shot" hit me again. When I was growing up, my dad had always talked about opening an Italian beef and hot dog joint as a business in Chicago. It seemed like every decent Italian family in the city did that; must be in the genes or something. At any rate, I convinced him that opening one up at EIU, in a college town where everyone was from the Chicago area, would be a great idea. I secured a lease at a fantastic location on Main Street, just across the street from the heart of the campus, and opened up "Joey's Place."

It was actually a pretty cool little place, with seating for twenty-five, your typical red and white checkered Italian theme, with a dancing hot dog as a logo. We delivered hot dogs, beef sandwiches, and pizzas all over campus. Joey's was a big hit from the day it opened, and I was personally featured as the student-businessman in interviews and local newspapers. That gave me quite the ego trip.

I was really proud of Joey's. It was my first real business, with ten employees, payrolls, sales taxes, vendor bills to cover, licenses and the health department to deal with. All got very real, real fast. Joey's took about $150,000 to open. I was proud of the way it looked, of the concept, and its creation, not to mention seeing my name in lights. The day they hung up the sign with the dancing hot dog, and the words "Joey's Place" lit up for the first time, I sat across the street with a cold beer in hand just looking at it well into the night.

But, as it turns out, I love the creation of concepts a lot more than the day-to-day operations. The actual business and cash flow wasn't the problem. The problem with Joey's Place was Joey; how I conducted myself and how I failed to operate the store as a business. It was simply a case of too much too soon, without learning the underlying respect for how I got it. Joey's place allowed me to play the "Big Shot" and helped me with something that I'd failed to do back in high school, and that was to fit in.

I was constantly giving away things to the cool crowd. After a night out, after the campus bars closed at two in the morning, I'd bring my new "friends" over to Joey's and fire up the grills. No, I certainly never operated Joey's as a business, and I have many regrets for that. But then again, I was never really taught what a business actually was. A business isn't just the concept, or walking around proudly puffing your chest out; a business is all the work you do to *earn* that right for puffing out your chest.

I had the right concept at the right place and time, but once all that was laid in my lap I failed miserably at the execution. I just never took it seriously. And, why would I? My ignorant view was that I had what I had, and was doing what I thought I was entitled to. Was I wrong…? Answer: HELL YEAH…!

Joey's Place made a lot of cash. And despite my frivolous ways, I managed to spend some of it wisely. I bought a few houses on campus and rented them out to junior and senior girls, and even managed to open up a tanning salon and clothing boutique that also turned out pretty well. It was called "The Body Shop", and I ended up selling it a few years later to a wide receiver on the EIU football team.

That "Big Shot" thing went straight to my head. I stopped paying attention to the details, and blew through money like a fool. More importantly, I was blowing opportunity. It still feels very unsettling even to this day.

How unsettling? This is best explained with a short but relevant sidebar. I opened up Joey's Place next door, at the *same time*, as another college restaurant shop opened. If I ran short on bread or some other item, I'd just run over and get some from the other owner, and reciprocate the next time he ran short on something.

Both of us were just a couple of college-age businessmen starting out at the same time. Both of us seemed to just be clawing to get a piece.

After I left EIU, many years later, I happened to see a NASCAR event on television and noticed that one of the racecars was sponsored by that same little sandwich shop that had been next door to Joeys Place. You may have even heard of it, considering that "Jimmy John's" has exploded into a coast-to-coast national chain.

Yeah, *that* Jimmy John's. I was happy for him at first, and thought it was pretty cool that I knew Jimmy when he was just starting out. But then I got to thinking…

Joey's Place started at the exact same time and the exact same place as Jimmy John's, and yet Jimmy John's went nationwide while Joey's Place stalled.

That was enough to make me feel like a failure.

Joey's Place was far from a failure, though. After nearly three years of me "running" the store, I sold it to the original managers of Jimmy John's and am proud to say that still to this day, some twenty-five years plus later, it's still there, in the same location I originally selected. And, now with three other locations. Joey's is still using the same dancing hotdog logo and the same color schemes. In fact, every now and then I'd call their number in Charleston just to hear them say, "Joey's Place, can I help you?"

With Joey's Place sold on contract, The Body Shop tanning and boutique store sold to that wide receiver, and all the campus houses I owned rented out, I went home to my parents' house for the summer. It was only a matter of days before I was bored and realized that I had a love for landscaping. Don't ask me why. So, I took a job with the same landscaping company that my parents used to maintain their own yard.

Here I was, back from "college", I'd owned and operated a couple successful businesses and was still getting rent from several pieces of real estate. Even with the things I had done at that stage, I was at my parents' home deciding to cut lawns for the summer… my parents' lawn, to boot. Go figure.

One hot day in late June I was cutting my parents' lawn with a crew of illegal immigrant workers that I was managing. At this point, my parents were doing quite well and had moved into a real nice neighborhood in the suburbs.

For me to work for this company, I had to wear an "official" landscaping uniform. It was the sort of neighborhood filled with judges, doctors, lawyers, business owners, and other professionals. A nice, respectable, neat-as-a-pin neighborhood with perfectly manicured lawns. And here I was the "successful" son who came back from college to do the manicuring in a God-awful green landscape jumpsuit. Mowing my own *parents'* lawn. Something to really be proud of, right?

I was in front of the house when the garage door opens. My Dad was pulling out. He was in a new car, all dressed up and ready to drive to his office. He noticed me taking equipment off the landscaping truck. That was it. He stopped the car and lowered the window to speak to me.

"This is what I paid for you to go to college for?"

That look in his eyes was like a knife to the heart. I never wanted to see that look again. I decided right then and there that I had to have it all right *now!* That look subconsciously planted the notion in me to reach success at all costs. As fate would have it, the next week my parents threw the party at their house that gave me an introduction to Tony Stack and my start at CBOT.

Chapter Four:

Gambling Made Easy

The technology of 1993 was nowhere close to what is possible today. Access to sports betting lines, line movements, and information was a challenge. It seemed like Benny was operating his ASU bookmaking business mainly from betting lines he would find in the papers, then adjusted those lines based on his own personal perception of whom he thought his customers would be betting on.

For example, he knew that certain groups of his campus customers would always bet with their hearts. So if he knew a certain customer was from NY, and that the New York Giants were playing, Benny would bump that betting line to his advantage. If the *true* Vegas betting line had the Giants as a 2.5 point favorite, then Benny might give that same game betting line out to his customers with the Giants as a *six* point favorite, or even higher. He knew his customers didn't care and that they certainly weren't smart enough to see what was going on.

It was a Mickey Mouse bookmaking operation that nonetheless offered college kids some betting action.

One day my brother's ASU roommate called me in Chicago and asked which teams I liked in the upcoming weekend games. He wanted a few good picks, and as I discovered, he really *needed* a few good picks. It turned out that he was a customer of Benny's and was down a lot of money and in desperate need of a few winners.

That week I really liked the Chicago Bears and was betting on them pretty heavily myself, with the Bears as a 2.5 to 3 point favorite. So I asked him to read me the betting lines he was getting from Benny, and when he did… well, all I could say was, *"Wow!"*

The betting lines Benny was giving out were completely jacked up. It seemed like he was taking every big city team east of ASU and recklessly bumping the betting lines in those games to his advantage.

As he read those lines to me, that particular weekend there were three to four games where Benny's lines were at least *four* points higher than the *true* Vegas line. For the Bears alone, Benny had them as an eight-point favorite. That was *five* points higher than Las Vegas. Now, five points may not seem like a lot to most people, but in football, when you're passing through numbers like 3, 4, 6, and 7, those numbers tilt the scales in *really* big ways.

Being the consummate gambling entrepreneurial fool that I was, rather than simply giving my brother's roommate a few lopsided picks so he could win back some of his money, I had to push the envelope, and regrettably began to think big again. So, I asked him to set me up a betting account directly with Benny's operation under a different name. I told him to just tell Benny that I was a childhood friend of his, that I had a great job, and needed higher betting limits if he wanted to take my betting action. My brother's roommate did as I asked, and soon I had a betting account inside Benny's bookmaking operation.

I was given limits of $5000 per game on straight bets, and $1000 limits on any parlays. With the inflated betting lines that Benny was giving out, in just six weeks, I completely annihilated his operation. The lowest weekly figure that I beat him for was around $20,000, with the highest around $65,000. To Benny's credit, though, I got paid every week, though don't ask me where he got the money, because I didn't care; every week I won, I got paid.

It wasn't too long, though, before the gossip leaked out as to who the mystery player with the killer winning streak was, and one day while I was at home in Chicago I got a call from Benny.

"Man, Joey, how on *Earth* are you ripping me apart here? Six weeks *straight* and I'm bleeding green."

"Benny," I told him, "I'll be honest with you. Your betting lines are simply jacked up. Where do you get them from anyway?"

"Well… As long as we're being honest, there's this other book operation on campus. All I try to do with my operation is lay off most of the action I take in so that I don't have the risk, and just focus on making the juice from my players."

"Oh really? Hmm… Benny, I may have an idea…"

It was on that phone call that we brainstormed a little arrangement that was of the "if we can't beat them, join them" variety. Benny opened up an account for me directly with his layoff operation in Tempe, and managed to get me even higher betting limits per game; $10,000 per game on straight bets, and $5000 on parlays. I guess you can imagine the mayhem that was in store for those people.

With the new account Benny had set up for me, the *same* results happened. Every week I beat them down and crushed them like a bug underfoot, and every week they paid me in *cash.* So much so that I had to fly my brother back and forth to Chicago to help deliver the money. There were several weeks during that 1993 football season when my weekly figures with that account exceeded $100,000. With the tilted edge I had on the games I played, it was just way too easy.

For many of the games I placed bets on, because of the difference in the betting lines, I had no risk *at all,* and would only bet the other side in hopes of having the game's final score fall in between the two numbers I bet so that I would "middle" the game and win *both* sides of the bet. It seemed so easy it was almost comical. To me it looked like legalized theft. My only problem was trying to find places to put the cash.

Still, all during the 1993 football season, I did the right thing and cut Benny in on my windfalls. In fact, we ended up developing a pretty good mutual trust between us. So much so that sometimes he would call me up just to BS on life, the markets, and personal relationships.

In my mind we weren't friends in the true sense of the word, but business partners. It was a friendship born in our pocketbooks and nurtured by corruption. We were basically just companions in crime, nothing more.

Chapter Five:

The Art of the F-I-X

Around mid-January of 1994, after the regular NFL football season had ended and before the Super Bowl, my home phone rang. It was Benny.

At that time I was living on the fourteenth floor of a really nice high-end luxury building just outside Chicago. I was in my home office talking to Benny about the usual nonsense when out of the blue he starts asking me about other bookmaking relationships I have and how much of a bankroll I had to play with. He was basically asking me how much money I had, and I thought that was really odd.

I still go back over that conversation in my mind. I was using a white portable home phone, sitting on my office chair behind my desk, looking out at the beautiful fresh snow coating the Chicago landscape. I remember being happy. It was a good day, and I was in a good place, when suddenly Benny springs it on me.

"Joey, I have a fix in play."

"Huh? I mean, yeah, okay."

I really had *no* idea what he was talking about and just tried to play it cool. I don't think it was hard for him to pick up on my confusion, though.

"A fix, yeah... Okay."

"No, Joey. I have a *fix*."

Then as clear as any thought in my mind still remains, he *literally* spelled out the letters.

"F… I… X!"

He said each letter slowly, over enunciating them in an effort to hammer them through to my brain.

It took a moment for it to sink in and really click in my mind before I could reply.

"A fix… Oh, a *fix!* Really?! How is that possible?"

"Ever heard of a player on the ASU men's basketball team by the name of Stephen 'Hedake' Smith?"

"No, can't say as I have." I said…

"Well, Hedake is the team's starting guard. Now, ASU is having a pretty good year as it is but Hedake is an absolute basketball *stud*. I mean, he'll go pro. He already leads the NCAA in minutes played, led the NCAA in three-point shots tried and made, is a PAC-10 all defensive player, and leads the PAC-10 in free throws. Joey, I'm telling you Hedake *is* the team; he dictates all that happens for his team during a game."

"He sounds like quite the baller, but where does the 'fix' come in?"

"Hedake plays more than just basketball, my man. He's a gambler and a customer of my bookmaking operation, and during the course of the past football season lost some *big* money betting. Even with what he's managed to pay me, he still owes me over twenty thousand dollars from betting losses and has *no* idea how he's going to pay me off. Hedake's only idea was to tell me that he could pay me off in full once he gets drafted to the NBA and goes pro. But, I had another idea."

Any person who had a proper moral compass, with no grey areas, would have hung up the phone right then and there, but Benny had me hooked. I was smart enough to know where this was going, but at this point in my life I felt bulletproof. Besides, I had been making a ton of money with Benny over the past year, and he had done right by me.

I let him continue…

"I whipped up a really good story for old Hedake and told him that the *real* owner of my bookmaking operation is an Italian family in Chicago with Mob ties, and that if I'm not able to collect that twenty grand then they would have to collect it themselves. And that would make things pretty ugly for all concerned."

"Benny, you're telling me that I'm supposed to be this Mob boss to you? And this idiot actually believes it?"

"Just wait and hear me out, will 'ya? Hedake bought it hook, line, and sinker; and I was able to convince him that the only way of wiping out his debt and making a few extra bucks in the process was for him to fix a couple of games. Oh, he was very resistant at first and kept pushing back that he would never lose any games on purpose, and all that trash, but I told him that he didn't need to lose anything. Instead of throwing the game, he simply must not win by any more points than I tell him to win by."

"And he bought it?" I said…

"Man, it's the perfect solution. As long as he doesn't have to out-and-out lose, – he's all in. He gets out of the mess he's in, pays off his debt, makes a few extra bucks in the process, and *we* make a killing. What could go wrong?"

Yeah, what could go wrong? I thought. I painfully chuckle now at that statement.

"I don't know, Benny," I hesitantly replied. "I mean, how could any-one, even Hedake, control any game in a way to dictate a win by a certain number of points?"

"Joey, this guy is *good*. He's a basketball surgeon."

"I'm not sure. If I'm going to bankroll this plan, I need to be a lot more convinced of Hedake's willingness and 'surgical' ability to perform." I said...

"Okay then, tell you what. I'll set up a call between you two so you can get a better feel for him. How's that sound?"

"Well, it's a start...and I get to play your fictitious Mob- connected guy? That should be some fun."

"*Now* you're getting the idea."

I remember that first conversation with Hedake like it was yesterday, and boy did he sound scared. For all he knew I *was* some Mob figure out of Chicago whom he owed money to, and if he didn't perform he would feel the results of my displeasure. We got on the phone the very next day. After a couple of pleasantries, Hedake got right to the point.

"I'll fix just two games for you," he said.

"Only two?" I asked. "What's the matter, you gonna find your moral compass then?"

"Oh no, sir, not- I mean, only two because I'll need to turn up my game and play hard for the NBA scouts again. I still need to keep my future NBA career in mind, you know."

"Sounds fair enough. Then you'll do it?"

"I'll... I'll do this, and make sure we don't win by more than what you tell me to. But, I will *not* lose any games."

I swear I could hear him sweating through the phone line, but after he committed and said what I needed to hear, I finally gave him some relief.

"Done," I said, "that's all you need to do. Let me look at the remaining schedule, then I'll get back to Benny with the games I think are the best spots for us to do this."

"Thank you, sir. Yes, sir."

That call made me a bit more comfortable. I felt we actually had a chance of pulling this off, so I gave Benny the green light. Now that I agreed to move forward with this scheme, Hedake went out and recruited Isaac Burton; the other guard on the ASU basketball team. With Isaac on board, we had *both* of the guards on the payroll. The way I figured, according to the ASU team numbers, I now had control of about 40% of the points that ASU was averaging per game that season.

Not only did I control most of the points being scored, but I also controlled whom the ball ended up going to as well. All of which greatly increased the odds for success in this scheme that would soon grow into one of the largest sports betting scandals of the modern era.

A couple of days after I told Benny the plan was a go, he tried several times to tell me that Hedake managed to get the starting center, Mario Bennett, involved in the plan as well. That was never proven to me, even after I talked about it with Hedake. Looking back, I think Benny attempted to put Bennett's name into the mix just to try and get more payoff money out of me, or maybe he was just trying to make me feel more secure about things.

I told Benny that I would make a $50,000 payment to Hedake for each game he fixed. Then out of that $50,000, Hedake would have to pay any other players he brought in. I just didn't want any BS down the road about him needing more money to get another player involved, so I wanted to make sure that the dollar amount was capped. Benny told Hedake that he would wipe out his remaining gambling debt as a bonus.

With two of the best players on board, I had to figure out which games we could hit, so I looked at the remaining ASU home games. ASU was having a pretty good year, but I needed to pick home games so ASU would be more likely to be a double digit favorite to win the game in the betting lines. The ASU basketball coach at the time was Bill Frieder, and many people thought he was leading that team as a lock selection for the NCAA's March Madness tournament.

I looked through the remaining schedule and saw a couple weeks down the road a Thursday/Saturday grouping of home games on the schedule. ASU was hosting Oregon State on Thursday, and then Oregon a couple days later on Saturday.

Looking at the win/loss records for the Oregon teams that year, with ASU at home, and knowing how well ASU had been playing, even though the games were still a couple of weeks away, I felt pretty comfortable that ASU would be a double digit favorite in the betting lines of *both* of those games.

But the final cherry on top was the date. When I saw how those games and dates lined up, it was like destiny itself was calling to me, beckoning me onward. Staring right back at me from that schedule was the ultimate prize, the gambler's holy day. The day that would take this modest scam and turn it into a multi-million dollar payday.

Super Bowl weekend.

Chapter Six:

The First Game

The first game I picked was on Thursday, January 27th, 1994. It was a home game for ASU vs. Oregon State. A couple of days before the game, I was able to get a pretty tight early range on what the projected betting line would be, with all indications showing that ASU would be a 13 to 13½ point favorite to win the game. I told Benny to set up another call for me to speak with Hedake directly before I started spending any money.

I was feeling a lot more confident and secure about our plans on that call. So much so that I actually tried to deepen my voice a bit as if I was the stereotypical Italian "Mobster" trying to scare someone. I laugh now thinking about it. Maybe I should have used the name "Guido" just to put it over the top, but that would have been a bit much.

"Hedake," I told him, "let me make this *very* clear."

"Yes, sir?"

"You need to perform in this coming Thursday's game. You can win the game, but the game *has* to land on a six. No more, no less."

In my mind, if the betting line was going to be around 13, I had to give Hedake a margin of error, so that if he missed six by a basket or two, and if the game happened to land on 10, then I would still be able to win my bets.

"I'll do it, sir. Six on the button. Exactly as you say."

With Hedake in place, I felt all was good to go on the game. Now all I needed was to set up the betting end of things to lay off as much money as I could without anyone knowing what I was doing. My goal was to open up new bookmaker betting accounts with different operations in the Midwest and East Coast. I pushed to get accounts opened with anyone I could find who would give me betting limits north of $10,000 per game. Between opening the new accounts and getting all of the liquid cash I could get together for my trip to Vegas to bet the game, the couple of days before the game were very busy ones for me, indeed.

I managed to recruit a guy I knew in Chicago by the name of Joe Mangiamele. Joe and his family owned and operated a third generation trucking company, one that was contracted to provide trucks to the City of Chicago. They had many relationships, most of which were dirty ones, so I used those "dirty" relationships to open up as many new bookmaking accounts as I possibly could to maximize the betting on the games. I wanted to spread out my betting action outside of Vegas to remain under the radar.

I booked my flight that Wednesday to leave for Vegas the next day. Thursday was the day of the game, with tipoff at 7pm MST. But when I woke up Thursday morning in Chicago, the city was literally bound down in an ice storm. The roads were closed, the airport at a standstill, and there was no way anyone was going anywhere anytime soon.

If this was God's way of telling me not to go… I didn't listen.

I had managed to get a little over $500,000 in cash to take with me to Vegas, and I set up fifteen different bookmaker accounts to bet with as well.

I'd arranged for a limo to pick me up at my house by 9AM, so that I could make the 11AM flight to Vegas. My anxiety was almost unbearable. With the storm nearly shutting the roadways down, the limo was late—very late.

When the limo finally picked me up, I sat in the back with a bag full of cash getting a bit pissy with the driver because I thought I was going to miss my flight and be forced to miss this chance after all my "work" already placed.

The $500,000 cash, Hedake, Benny, the fix, the profits, the book-making accounts, and the duffel bag, all with me trying to get to the airport. This entire setup was riding on me getting to the airport, and off to Vegas in time, during one of the worst storms of the year.

You might think I was nervous about getting $500,000 in cash through security, but the truth is I never thought twice about it. I'd already been making trips to Vegas with $100,000 plus, so carrying a large amount of cash was nothing new to me. Besides, it wasn't like it was against the law. I was headed to Vegas. What could the authorities do?

I finally did get to the airport. With only minutes to spare, I did my best OJ Simpson impression to make it to the gate on time, weaving through crowds, leaping over luggage, and almost doing a duck and roll under and around one obstacle after another. I was in a race, about to near the finish line of my gate, when I saw the announcement.

All flights were delayed.

It was the storm; too much ice on both the runways and the wings of the airplanes.

"No no no, this *can't* happen!"

But it had. The best and only idea I could come up with was to call my dad from an airport payphone and do my best to try and explain to him what I was doing. Looking back now, I really wish my dad hadn't answered that call.

A few years earlier, in 1990, my parents had moved to Las Vegas to retire. My dad loved Vegas, and had some gamble in him, but was clueless about sports betting and had no idea of how sports betting lines worked. So there I was, on a public payphone at O'Hare Airport, with a duffle bag filled with a half million dollars in cash hanging around my shoulders, trying to convince my then sixty-year old dad to leave his house ASAP, go to the bank, take out every penny he could, and bet on a college basketball team named Oregon State plus the points.

"And you have to do it *now,* Dad, because the game's in about six hours."

That was one frustrating call, let me tell you, but my dad always believed in me. I bit my lip, trying to be patient while my dad took notes on everything I told him so that he could understand what to do. He finally agreed to help me in my bind and do it all as I'd instructed.

Reflecting on what I now know transpired next, I wish he'd questioned me then, or at least said, "No, Joey. What you're doing is wrong and I want no part of it."

I would have probably been pissed that day- maybe even for a few months. But, the course of my life would have gone very differently if my dad had put his foot down.

To be clear: I don't blame him, of course. I take full ownership of my choices made. But, looking back, I honestly don't think at that point my dad really understood what I was doing was wrong. My dad's no dummy, but he wasn't a sports guy. He loved gambling, but black jack and slots were more his thing. I doubt he knew that sports games could be fixed. He took my call and probably just thought it was like some type of bond trade I wanted to do: he didn't understand it, but if I thought it was a good idea then, so did he.

I often think of that call with my dad now when I parent my own children. My only hope is they not only learn from my past, but listen to me more than I did to my dad.

Looking back with regret is a waste of thought, of course, because my dad agreed to help. I told him to gather up a friend or two because I knew he'd need help getting the money together and making those kinds of bets.

I didn't want him betting over $10,000 in any one casino under one name. Anytime a person bets over $10,000 in one spot in *cash*, on a single ticket, the casino will make you fill out a Currency Transaction Report, a "CTR" form. That report then triggers a red flag warning to the IRS about the person who bet the cash, so that the IRS can then examine that person's tax returns to see if he had enough income to justify his actions.

I didn't want my dad to put his name on those BS government forms and get caught in any crosshairs, so that's why I told him to get a couple of friends together to help him out, and warned him about the max betting amount.

Even though the flight was delayed, my plane finally took off from Chicago, landing me in Vegas around four in the afternoon. My Dad and his friends, Jimmy Nuzzo and Peter DiSilvestri, picked me up curbside at the airport, with my duffle bag full of cash.

The three of them had already managed to bet about $80,000 before I got into town, and much to my amazement, all the tickets were done right, too. Together, the four of us started to make the rounds to the big hotels to bet the remaining money I had with me.

The group of guys my dad pulled in resembled the characters from *Ocean's Eleven*. Jimmy was a trumpet player for Tom Jones and had some pretty *crazy* stories, and one of the most obnoxious laughs you'll ever hear. Peter was an old commodities trader from Chicago, who in his day had big money and a large firm of his own but managed to lose it all. Between these two characters and my Dad, the laughter was endless.

No time to laugh now. With about three hours until game tipoff and we had about $420,000 to bet on a Thursday night college basketball game, not to mention the calls I needed to make to the fifteen bookmakers that I'd opened accounts with in the Midwest and East Coast. With time running out, I came up with the best plan that I could.

"Dad, I'm giving you, Jimmy, and Peter a hundred thousand each in cash." I said…

"That's a lot of money, Joey. Are you sure this is okay?"

"I got this handled, Dad… believe me. Now I need you three to separate so we can move faster, and each make their own bets. Got it?"

He nodded.

"Dad, right now I need you to drop me off at Bally's. After you've all done the betting, come back with the completed tickets, and meet me back at Bally's. Remember…no more than ninety-nine hundred on any one ticket."

At $9900 per place, splitting up was the only way I was ever going to bet my full $500,000. As for myself, I kept the remaining $120,000 to bet for myself. I decided to hit Bally's, Barbary Coast, and a little sportsbook place called Little Caesars. The place is gone now, but back then it was located in a strip mall where the Paris Hotel now stands. The place was owned and operated by Gene Mayday, a *true* gambler. His motto for that operation of his was, "If you can bring it, I'll take it."

I got lucky that late afternoon connecting with Gene and was able to bet approximately $80,000 of my money at Little Caesars and never had to fill out a CTR form. The rest of the money I got off between Bally's and Barbary Coast.

With all my cash bet, and Dad and his friends handling their parts, I checked in at Bally's and went up to my room so I could make the phone calls I needed to complete all the bets with the fifteen bookmaker accounts. I called all fifteen and bet a minimum of $10,000 on the game straight, along with Oregon State in a few chosen parleys as well.

After calling the bookmakers, I made a quick call to Benny back in Arizona.

"Benny, what's happening over there?"

"I'm on my way to watch the game in person. I'm going to sit right behind the ASU bench so I can make sure that Hedake sees me and remembers what he's supposed to be doing."

"Everything's good with Hedake?" I said…

"Don't worry, it's all good! I spoke with Hedake a couple hours ago after their pre-game shoot around. He's well aware of what needs to be done. Just sit back and *feel* the money.

Around 6:30, shortly before tipoff, I met with my Dad, Jimmy, and Peter at the sportsbook inside Bally's. They'd all done a great job and successfully bet the $100,000 I'd given each of them.

I organized all the tickets in envelopes. Each one had the tickets inside for the specific hotel they'd been bet at, and on the outsides of each one I wrote a breakdown of the tickets inside, as well as the amounts that would need to be collected at that casino when cashed in.

When betting this kind of money, using over two dozen different locations and involving people at the last minute, organization is vital. I collected all their tickets, added in the ones I'd personally bet, and put them in a safe deposit box at Bally's.

The deal I made with Benny was that I would pay him personally $50,000 to $100,000 per game, the number depending on how much action I was able to get off, though I always knew full well I was only going to give him a *maximum* of $50,000 per game, along with the $50,000 I'd agreed to pay Hedake.

Greed, laced with larceny opened the door to leaving out some details…lying to your partner. I felt comfortable not giving him the full story of how much I was betting, how many bookmakers I was betting with, or what I'd brought with me to Vegas to bet. My basic plan on handling Benny was that, no matter how much I managed to bet or win, he should be thankful if I gave him $50,000 per game. My justification was he had no skin in the game; it was my money at risk if things went south.

No honor among thieves.

In addition to the $500,000 in cash that I'd brought, and the fifteen bookmaker accounts I was betting with, I'd also brought another $25,000 of side money as well. 'Play money,' if you will. I figured that *if* the ASU game lost the bet on Thursday night, then I'd most likely be staying in Vegas for the weekend anyways. And besides, it was Super Bowl weekend. If you are in Vegas on Super Bowl weekend it's best to have a few extra bucks on you.

But, with nearly $800,000 now bet on a game set to start in about 20 minutes, that 'play money' was starting to burn a hole in my pocket. So at twenty minutes before tipoff, I looked into maximizing my profits for this extra $25,000.

I started betting a flurry of $2000 parlays, each one keying Oregon State plus the points in all of them. Then, for the other team needed in the parley, I would use *both* teams that were playing against one another, but only if that point spread was even numbered with *no* half points. For example, if the Bulls were playing the Knicks, and the Bulls were a four-point favorite to win the game. I would make a $2000 parley with Oregon State plus the points as my *key* team, and the Bulls minus the four points. Then, the same parlay with Oregon State as the key, but this time with the Knicks plus the four points.

This way, as long as Hedake and ASU did their jobs and didn't cover the spread, I was guaranteed $5200 back on every $2000 bet. It was a true two times plus on every dollar bet without having to pay the "juice" to Vegas in the process.

I only picked games in the parlay to go with the Oregon State game with even numbered point spreads, because *if* that second game ended up landing directly on the spread number, then provided that Hedake did *his* job as needed, both of the $2000 parlays I bet would revert to single team bets. That basically means that I'd win on *both* tickets bet. It was a beautiful plan.

Everything now rested on Hedake's performance.

Usually for any Thursday night college basketball game, betting any remotely sized *big* action is pretty difficult to hide without alerting anyone as to what you're doing, or changing the betting line.

Superbowl weekend was the *perfect* weekend to do this.

Super Bowl weekend: the Dallas Cowboys were playing the Buffalo Bills. There was a *ton* of money in Vegas that weekend, and because of that it allowed my money to remain under the radar. Even with all of the "out of the ordinary" betting on a somewhat meaningless Thursday night ASU game, after all the money I bet was in place, at one point I'd only moved the line down to ASU minus ten. When that happened, there were enough people, action, and money in Vegas that others would bet on ASU and moving the number back the other way.

It couldn't be more *perfect*.

With $500,000 cash bet in Vegas on Oregon State plus the points, straight bets and many parley bets with fifteen bookmakers in the Midwest and on the East Coast for a minimum of $10,000 per game, and the $25,000 in funky parlay action I bet at Bally's before the tipoff, my "work" was done, and it was time to watch the game. The only problem was the game wasn't being shown anywhere in Vegas, so my Dad and his two friends and I sat in the Bally's sportsbook, ate hotdogs, drank a few drinks, and watched a sports ticker scroll by with the game updates every ten to fifteen minutes.

The betting line on the game opened with ASU as a 13 to 13½ point favorite, but we were able to get the overwhelming majority of the betting action done at around Oregon State plus 12 to 12½. The line dipped down to ASU minus 10 at one point, but the unsuspecting public came in and bet on ASU, moving the line the other way again thinking there was value. The Super Bowl money in Vegas made sure that my money bet stayed well hidden.

All that remained was for Hedake and Burton to earn their money by not covering the spread. Then, I would collect.

For the next two and a half hours, the four of us sat in Bally's sportsbook patiently waiting and watching the sports ticker for game updates. For most of the first half, the updates showed ASU leading by double digits—not good. I knew that Oregon State had one of the worst teams in the Pac-10 that year, so if ASU got on a roll, then I knew that Hedake, Burton, or even an act of God wouldn't be able to save my money. By halftime ASU was clearly in control of the game.

Early in the second half, the ticker scrolled showing ASU with a 13-point lead, and I thought for sure my money was in serious trouble. At the 10-minute mark into the second half, ASU still had a strong double digit lead.

Then, the "magic" started to happen.

Update after update showed the ASU lead dwindling down, until *finally* the final score flashed. Sure enough, Hedake and Burton both did their jobs. ASU had won the game, but only by six. The final score was 88 to 82; it had landed on a *SIX*. It was amazing!

The number was *exactly* what I'd told Hedake it needed to be. Crazy what two players can do to direct and dictate a game's outcome, and what money can make people do. I still wish that I had been able to see the final ten minutes of play in person.

Shortly after the game ended I was able to reach Benny by phone. With a "winner" now in the books, I continued to downplay to him the amounts I was able to bet. I told him how difficult it was for me to bet since I didn't want to move the betting line and alert anyone to what I was doing.

Then he told me about the game.

"Joey, I tell 'ya, if I wasn't at the game seeing it for myself, I'd *never* have believed it! Hedake had his best game ever. Scored 28 points in the first half. And, 39 for the game. He hit 10 -3 pointers. The kid was in a complete zone offensively"

When he told me this, I couldn't believe what I was hearing. 39 points! I thought this guy was on our side?

Then, Benny went on to explain.

"The last ten minutes was like a choreographed play. ASU was easily a twenty-point or better team than Oregon State. But with only a few minutes left on the clock, Hedake was like a raging bull on a mission. He *took over* the game, because he knew that if it didn't land on a six, he wasn't gettin' paid. Man, it was beautiful."

What most people don't get is that a "fix" or "point shaving" in a game isn't about a poor offensive performance. A true "FIX" is done by manipulating the game with little twists that the unsuspecting public won't notice. Players on "the take" can just allow opposing players to put points on the board by backing up a step or two on defense, or giving them an edge by simply not interfering with what the other team does offensively. That's all Hedake had to do that night. And, he did it to perfection.

Because in the end, all the general public cares about is the win. Everyone *loves* a winner, and ASU's fan base didn't care about what Hedake didn't do because he *rocked* the house that night in ASU's home building. He torched the nets with 39 points, and personally stole all the headlines the next day. All the while *no one* even suspected what was going on behind the scenes. That was the kind of talent this kid had.

One of my favorite lines in the movie "*A Bronx Tale*" occurs when Robert De Niro's character breaks down life to his son and says to him that the saddest thing in life is "wasted talent." On reflection, I can't help but think about Hedake, and how he wasted his talent for money. I often think where he would be, had I not influenced him to make this fateful decision...a decision that would end his career before it started.

After I spoke with Benny, my fun was just getting started. My dad and I spent the next few hours driving around Vegas stopping at over twenty casinos and various sportsbooks cashing the tickets bet on the game. I had a *great* time with my dad that night, and it's a memory I still cherish.

In Vegas alone that night, my dad and I collected a little over $1.1 million in cash. Then, when I calculated all the winning figures with the fifteen bookmaker accounts, I had an additional $400,000 plus to collect on. Even my funky parlays at Bally's made me a little over $60,000.

$1,560,000 in total. Not a bad day at all…

I had all this money in cash, carrying it around in a duffle bag like a bag of clothes. My dad and I simply walked from casino to casino cashing tickets and no one knew a thing. I wore a basketball cap and a pair of jeans, so I looked like I didn't have two nickels to rub together… just a duffle bag *filled* with hundred dollar bills.

It was definitely a pretty cool night, and my dad and I had a lot of fun. At one point he said, "Joey, I just can't believe you can make this kinda money on a silly Thursday night college basketball game."

I told him, "Well Dad, we had the players."

He got it. All that cash—not some number in a bank account but real cash, *stacks* of hundred dollar bills—will do that to you. You justify it. Fast cash—huge amounts of it—is like a drug.

I guess right there he made his peace with it.

I didn't sleep much that Thursday night; I just kept replaying the events in my mind, trying to think of ways I could have done things better. My focus was now on getting Hedake to repeat the *same* performance for ASU's game on Saturday against Oregon, so I called Benny early Friday morning.

"Benny, jump on a flight and get here to Vegas ASAP!"

"Okay, my man, but what's the rush?"

"I want you to get Hedake's fifty thousand dollars in *cash,* so you can get it in his hands, by Friday. I think if Hedake has cash money in his hands overnight for one full day, and can feel that aura of power that comes with it, then my telling him to do a repeat performance on Saturday is a guarantee. Whatever he chooses to do with that money, or what he decides to pay Burton or maybe even Bennett, I don't care. My deal is with Hedake."

"Gotchya. Don't worry, by the time I'm finished he'll think he's dealing with Al Capone," Benny replied.

Hedake was a street kid from Dallas, so I knew that him holding that much actual *cash* overnight, and knowing that I did all that I said I was going to do, was going to be key for the success of Saturday's game. Once Hedake held that money in his hands, he was *mine*. Come Saturday, he would run through a wall for me if I needed him to.

It was like eating potato chips: when he had that money, I knew he couldn't fix just the *one* game. There would always be one more, and that way of thinking inevitably leads to the fall.

Chapter Seven:

The Perfect Weekend

That Friday around noon I went to McCarron Airport in Vegas to meet Benny. I was at the gate waiting for the plane to empty when I saw him walk out the jet way. I went over to him with the $50,000.

"Give this to Hedake," I told him.

"Will do," he replied, taking the package. "So, how much did you make on the game?"

"Around two hundred thousand,"

I lied. But I think Benny had to know it. He couldn't have been foolish enough to think I was doing this for just a couple hundred grand. Could he...?

"I had to be real careful not to attract any attention." I said...

"Not bad. How much you gonna pay me?"

"I'm gonna give you the fifty grand we discussed."

"Okay..."

Then he said something that gave me all the confidence I needed for Saturday.

"...Joe, why don't you take that fifty thousand that you're gonna give me and bet it on Saturday's game against Oregon for me. Because once I hand Hedake this fifty thousand in cash after his practice today, he's ours for Saturday."

That was what I wanted to hear, and boy did it ever make me smile! I knew I was on for another bite of the apple, and even after collecting over $1 million dollars on game one, I wanted to do it bigger and better this time.

Friday night in Vegas the early overnight betting lines were posted at some casinos for Saturday's college basketball games. ASU opened against Oregon as a 12 to 12½ point favorite. On overnight lines, only a few major hotels on the Strip will take bets on college basketball, and even the ones that do limit the betting amounts to around $2000 to $3000 per game. So, I had to be careful that night not to set off any alerts or move the betting line.

Friday afternoon I had Joe Mangiamele and his dad fly into Vegas to help. They already knew what I was doing, and I knew they were betting the game anyways, so I might as well use their help. This time around I figured I was going to need a lot of help spreading all this money around town. I bet around $100,000 on Oregon plus the 12 points on the overnight lines that Friday night.

Saturday morning was a different story, however. It was the day before the Super Bowl, so the Vegas sportsbooks were full of people and action. The Dallas Cowboys with Emmitt, Aikman, and Irvin were playing, so there was a *ton* of big Texas money and guys in business suits throwing it around. With that kind of money in town, it made it easy to do pretty much anything we wanted with the sportsbooks. But, before I went all-in and bet any more dollars on the game, I wanted to talk to Hedake one more time for myself. I had to make sure to hear from him directly that he was committed and all-in for the game later that day.

I talked to him late in the morning. I started off by congratulating him on what he did that Thursday, but was selective with my words, I didn't want to sound like the money mattered to me.

"Hey," I then asked, trying to sound as cool as I could, "did you get that, um, *package* I left with Benny for you the other day?"

"Oh, yes I did, sir. Thank-you, thank-you, thank-you. And don't worry about today. I'm your man." He replied.

"Not sure what you were thinking dropping 39 points the last game. You had me doubting you a little. Remember, Hedake, I need the game today to land on a six again, just as last time. Thursday's game made me very happy... you don't want to change that."

The betting line was actually at 12, but I again wanted that margin of error because I figured there was simply *no way* he could make it hit the *exact ending number* that I told him to hit twice.

"Okay yes sir, of course not, sir. Six it'll be. It won't be an issue at all, sir. I got you handled on this."

When I hung up with him, I *knew* I was right; his attention to what I said, and reaction to questions I asked, proved all that I suspected. That $50,000 in cash that sat in his hands overnight grew its own greedy conscience. I think if I'd asked him that day to make sure ASU didn't score, he would have fought that fight too. That kid would have done just about anything I asked at that point.

The game for that Saturday, January 29th, 1994, against Oregon was set for a late tipoff, so that gave me most of the day to bet the game in a more efficient way. My dad was with me again, and now I had Joe Mangiamele and his father along helping to make the bets as well.

Together I ended up betting a little over $1.2 million on Oregon plus the points, not to mention whatever the Mangiameles brought with them as well; God only knows what the two of them laid off with the bookmakers.

I again used over twenty casinos and random sportsbooks to make all the bets, and even a bunch of solo sportsbook joints, most of which aren't even open anymore. But even with all of that money we bet on a single, basically meaningless, regular Saturday college basketball game, I ended up hardly moving the betting line at all. The Super Bowl weekend fixed everything. I was truly flying under the radar. It all seemed so easy...

The bulk of the dollars bet were placed at the larger casinos in amounts no higher than $9900 per ticket. With four people in our group, we would wait in separate lines and each bet $9900. Because the sportsbooks were so packed that weekend, we'd each go to different tellers and get off another $9900. Betting $1.2 million, $9900 at a time; takes quite a bit of time…and nerve. Most of the spots I went to had limits of $5000. The only thing that saved us was the Super Bowl weekend. Each time my group would make a move to pound Oregon on a bet, thus moving the line some, the Texas big-money people in town would bet on ASU, thinking it was a steal at the newly discounted number, and move the line back for us the other way.

It was sort of like walking a tightrope, only in this case our balance bar was that Texas money and the hordes of sports fanatics in Vegas for a big game.

Betting and watching those lines was as almost as much of a rush as winning.

I finally finished betting all the money I had by about two in the afternoon. As before, I gathered up all the tickets, put them in individually labeled envelopes for each casino, locked them up in a safe deposit box at Bally's, and waited for the tipoff.

I bet a total of $1.2 million in Vegas that day on Oregon plus the points for this game, and another $300,000+ with the fifteen different bookmakers I'd opened accounts with. As before, I took the over $60,000 I'd created via the "funky" parleys from Game One and did the same structure for this game, but now using Oregon as the key team. In all, I was in about $1.6 million deep for this game and *needed* Hedake and Burton to perform as they had before.

Why go all in? Why not take a little money off the table after the success on Thursday night? I'll tell you why:

Because I had the players. The rush of "owning" the game was too intoxicating. With Thursday night's success and Hedake's ability to end on a specific number, it was almost as if I had an unlimited ATM card. I was paying to fix the game—I sure wasn't going to hold anything back.

Hold back? Not my style.

I knew by face, and a few by name, some of the key tellers, ticket writers, and supervisors at a few of the larger sportsbooks in town, and because of the action I played, house limits were mostly overlooked and I was well taken care of. Along the way, I'd also taken care of a few of them on the prior Thursday night game, telling them with a wink and a nod to bet everything they could on Oregon State.

That winner I gave a few of them from Game One, combined with my generous tipping, obliged some of the ticket writers and supervisors to take me aside and pass along to me some fairly upsetting news.

"Joe, there's a group of college age kids running around town betting on Oregon pretty hard as well." Then he said, "In fact, a few of the kids making the bets had ASU shirts on."

"Oh, really?" I said.

"I thought you should know this," he continued. "They're emptying their pockets betting with twenty dollar bills like they already know the final score."

It was all I could do to maintain a calm exterior after I heard this, but when I did, I knew that Benny had leaked the information out to others and sure wasn't being exclusive to me as he swore he was.

I was already all-in at this point, it was way too late to bitch and moan. This was supposed to be the last game, and I knew I was getting the better end of the plan. So, even though I was pissed, my attitude was basically, "So be it..."

The game tipped off later that night. Oregon was a much better team than Oregon State had been, but ASU and Hedake controlled the game in most areas and led the *entire* way. We watched the game at Bally's, and even though I knew what was going on, and how motivated I had made Hedake, watching the game on TV I knew it was being played just perfectly. There were even a couple of times when Coach Frieder tried to take Hedake out of the game, but Hedake just waived him off. Frieder was the coach. But, Hedake controlled the team.

Maybe it was the taste of money he got from me a day earlier. Or, maybe it was just an off night for him. But, Hedake only had 13 points. The points, -or lack thereof - didn't matter much. Everything else he dictated on the court that night made the difference. He was on a mission. There was *no way* he wasn't going to get the job done and get paid that night.

As it turns out, in the last ten minutes of this game, Hedake- an all PAC-10 defensive player of the year- clearly gave a few extra feet of space to the opposing player he was guarding. At that level, that's all that's needed to make the difference. Hedake was a 90%+ free-throw shooter, and yet he missed several free-throws down the stretch.

Then there were the turnovers. Simple inbound passes that ASU needed to make after an Oregon basket were tanked and tossed away. On a couple of plays, Burton would inbound the ball after an Oregon basket, Hedake would cut one way, and Burton would throw the ball behind him, thus turning the ball over and giving it right back to Oregon again.

The funny thing about watching this to me was Hedake's acting. It seemed like he felt compelled to stomp the floor or yell at his teammates after a bad pass or foul. Not only was Hedake fixing the game for me so it would land on six, but he was also selling what he was doing to his competitors, coaches, and fans as well.

Other than a few selective turnovers in the closing minutes of the game, Hedake and Burton were, to say the least, *masterful*. I'd strongly reminded him just earlier in the day that the game had to land on a six, but could he do it?

Yep... ASU won the game 84 to 78. For the second game in a row, he nailed it, winning by *SIX*. This time by having little to do offensively. Utterly *amazing!* That kid's talent was beyond belief.

Money...large amounts of money, always attracts the dark side of human nature—the fix. This is especially true in individual sports; the margin of victory at the top of any sport is so narrow that it's virtually impossible to tell when a guy isn't giving it his all. A favorite's performance could drop off a percent or two and suddenly he loses. And with that, could anyone at that point claim a fix? Not really, just things that make you wonder. Especially with large amounts of money on the line.

Team sports are harder to fix, but, as we've seen, it can be done. Just so many unknown variables that could mess things up. Coaches, and other player's self-serving interests could block the end success. Not to talk about fixing a game again, but I often think that the only team sport that could be truly fixed today is hockey. Give me a goalie willing to get paid, making sub-par bucks a year, in the twilight of his career. And, let me bet OVER the total for the game.

All he would need to do is let the first 3-4 shots on goal get past him in the first period, and basically it's a winner. In today's world, with the betting all around the globe, I could probably get off over ten million on a weekend game in the NHL. That will make you think…!!!

The point to ALWAYS remember is that real people are behind all these games, lines, and action. And where there's people and money, there's corruption. A good chance for it, in many cases.

After the game I talked to Benny. My attitude with him was different now because I knew he was playing me by letting others in on what I was paying for. But I'd just won a couple million bucks in cash for three days of 'work', and was probably not really going to need to speak to him again, so I didn't bother to bring anything up.

After all, I was still getting the better end of the deal and only giving him $50,000 per game. So with both games now done and officially winners, I was content to be happy, handle my remaining obligations with Benny and Hedake, and just move onward with my life.

I was a very happy twenty-five-year-old kid that Saturday night.

My Dad, the Mangiameles, and I spent the next two or three hours driving around Las Vegas to some twenty or so hotels and solo sportsbooks cashing in our winning tickets. When we were done, I had over $2.3 million in cash collected on straight bets made in Vegas, plus a little over $800,000 accumulated in positive balances with the fifteen bookmaker accounts. I'd also turned my original $25,000 of funky parlay money into a total of $150,000.

I raked in about $3.3 million in just three days.

The monetary intoxication was unbelievable.

After all the tickets were cashed in, and the money safely tucked away in a safe deposit box, I called Benny and told him to catch a flight to Vegas on Super Bowl Sunday so I could pay him the remaining money I owed him. With both games won and done, my goal was to settle obligations and close this chapter of my life. The way I pulled off those Thursday and Saturday games, with the help of the Super Bowl, was both lucky and masterful.

I was confident it went unnoticed.

At this point, even though I *knew* what I did was wrong, it was the furthest thing from my mind. I made more money that weekend than most people earned in a lifetime.

Sunday morning found me at the safe deposit box pulling out the money I needed to pay Benny plus the $50,000 I owed Hedake for his work on Game Two. I owed Benny the original $50,000 for Game One, along with the $45,000 he'd won betting on Game Two with Game One's money, and his regular $50,000 payment for that second game. In all, I pulled out $195,000 in stacks of $10,000 each to give to Benny, stuffed it all in my duffle bag, and went off to McCarron Airport to meet him for what I thought was the final time.

When I got to the gate, the plane emptied and Benny wasn't there. I called his apartment on Campus. His roommate Barry told me that he had been out late celebrating, missed the early flight, and should arrive in Vegas in about an hour. I decided to wait for him at his new arrival gate so that I could just end this saga.

With every passing second, I became more agitated.

While I was waiting there for him, I found my temper rising. Here

I was waiting at the airport to pay him *his* money, and he was late. I kept recalling what I'd heard from sportsbook people all over town that ASU students were emptying their pockets of twenty-dollar bills betting the game that *I'd* created the opportunity on and paid for.

It really pissed me off that Benny and others benefited behind my back for what I'd paid to make happen. More importantly, he had totally put the betting lines at risk with this leak. It could have tanked the entire deal. So as I stood there waiting, I stewed on this. Like an angry child, every few minutes I would reach into the duffle and take out random hundred dollar bills from his stacks and stuff them in my pocket. I did that and muttered profanities about him because of his telling others about what I paid for. Every minute of my wasted time I felt justified in penalizing him a few hundred dollars.

By the time he arrived, I handed him the bag with not a word exchanged between us. He knew what he was doing and what he'd pulled on me, and I knew the same on my side, so we both just let it go.

As I took my limo back to Bally's, I kept thinking that I would have loved to have a camera on him when he was finally alone to count that money I gave him, and to see the expression on his face when he realized that each of the $10,000 stacks was short by about $500 to $700. I felt justified. In fact, with all that loose talk, it could have been very serious. Had more people bet, it could have moved the line, or put the entire fix on the feds' radar. This was the last time, and I was out, so I wasn't worried.

Had I been the real gangster Benny presented to Hedake, Benny never would have opened his mouth. He'd have been too scared of the results.

In the end, Benny *never* said one word to me about giving the info out or the money being short. Who knows what he made on the other side. As much as it bothered me then, no honor among thieves worked both ways.

With all of my ASU work now over, and all the obligations involved handled, it was time to celebrate a little, and it couldn't have fallen on a better day. I was in Las Vegas, twenty-five, single and, oh yeah…I'd just profited a little over $2.5 million in cash. So my dad, the Mangiamele's, and I decided to go to a Super Bowl party Bally's was hosting at the hotel.

It was several celebratory drinks into the day, before the Super Bowl game had begun, when my dad ran into a friend he knew from Chicago by the name of Dominick Basso. Dominick had been on the wrong side of the law many times in his life, and was a very well-known bookmaker in Chicago. In fact, he's the very same bookmaker who took all of Pete Rose's betting action when he was a player and a manager. The feds had tried to take Basso down for years, but never got him with anything other than some little missteps along the way.

My Dad invited Dominick and his son Vince to join us at our reserved table to watch the game. Vince was about my age, and looking to follow in the footsteps of his father's career as a bookmaker.

We all bet the Cowboys pretty hard that day, myself to the tune of $220,000. As the game started and we all watched Buffalo beat up on Dallas in the first half, the drinks kept coming, and with those drinks came questions about what I had done the prior three days, so details of the events came out in the conversation.

The Bassos wanted in, and were upset with my dad and me that they hadn't known in advance. They said with the connections they had, that they could have moved *millions* on the game.

That thought was a nightmare to me. Even as the drinks numbed me somewhat, I kept thinking what would have happened if I'd gotten guys like that involved and the game tanked.

No question…with people like that involved, it would have been a bad situation for me if things went south.

At that moment, though, their whining about not being involved wasn't my problem. The games were over, I made some money, and they'd simply missed out. I owed them nothing.

"I only structured two games," I told them. "Sorry you missed out, but it's done and I'm out."

What I remember next is the Cowboys just dominating the second half of the game, and I was running all over the place drunkenly shouting, "How 'bout them Cowboys!"

In addition to the millions I cleared on the two fixed games, I cashed in my winning Super Bowl ticket for $420,000. What an amazing end to a historical weekend.

I flew back to Chicago with a total of about three million in cash. Back in those days, the authorities didn't care what you brought on a plane, so I walked right on with a duffle bag over my shoulder and no one thought twice about anything. For me, it had been the weekend of a lifetime. I was under the radar, no one suspected anything, and I'd made a *ton* of cash. Life couldn't be better.

I thought I was out. I planned on getting married, and using the dollars to get a jumpstart on trading, but greed *always* gets you in the end. With all that fast cash made, the grey areas I danced in were just selectively ignored.

Chapter Eight:

Playing Motivated

Once back in Chicago I returned to my life at the CBOT, keeping my mouth shut about everything that had happened. Life was going quite well until about two weeks later, on a Wednesday night, specifically February 16, 1994. I was at home and my phone rang.

It was Hedake.

"I was wondering, sir, if I could make a bet on myself through you to win the game we're scheduled to play tomorrow against UCLA?"

I froze.

Totally shocked by what he was saying, and even more shocked that he was even calling me direct with this BS. But I listened to him. He went on and on about how it was his senior year, and how in his four years at ASU they had never beaten UCLA. That year, as most years, UCLA was a real powerhouse. That team was *loaded*. They had "Big" George Zidek in the middle, and the O'Bannon brothers as the stars of the team. Not an easy team to beat.

As I was talking to him, I was on the computer checking a betting line source that I had. It showed that ASU was probably going to be around a four-point *underdog* at home against UCLA for this game. Now, in my mind I knew that I had just paid Hedake $100,000 in *cash* for his work in the two Oregon games three weeks earlier, but over the past couple of weeks I'd also heard many comments from my brother that Hedake was spending money around campus like crazy. I heard he'd bought a new truck, as well as a gold necklace with a basketball in diamonds. So, while I was talking to him, I asked him straight out.

"Why do you want to bet?"

"Well, sir, because I never beat them before." He said...

"And how much do you want to bet?"

"I want to win twenty thousand dollars."

"OK, but do you have the money to pay me if you lose?"

"Sir," he said very strongly, "I'm *not* gonna lose. *That* you can bet on."

"Okay," I finally told him. "You've got ASU plus four tomorrow night for twenty-two thousand dollars. We'll settle up the day after the game. Good luck."

I felt in my gut when I hung up the phone that Hedake was broke. That he'd spent all the money I'd given to him. And, if he lost this $22,000 bet to me the next day, I knew he would once again be in a really bad situation.

I also knew that the guys making the betting lines are *exceptionally* smart. Forget the earlier ASU games that I had *fixed* a couple weeks earlier. If the line makers were putting UCLA as a four point favorite on ASU's home court, with NCAA tourney implications on the line, it was a pretty safe assumption on my part that UCLA would be no pushover.

I figured that if Hedake lost his bet to me the next day in this game against UCLA, most likely he wasn't going to be able to pay me the $22,000. With that, I quickly assumed that the only way he would be able to get me my $22K would be to deliver another fix on the USC game coming up on Saturday, two days after UCLA.

So Thursday morning, the day of the UCLA game, I called in sick to work with Tony at the CBOT, and went to the bank to get $2.5 million in cash out of my safe deposit box and once again shoved it all into a duffle bag to board a flight to Arizona alone.

I wanted to personally be at and watch the ASU-UCLA game. I was real curious to see first-hand what a motivated and desperate player looked like.

I called Benny before I got on the plane to tell him what was going on, but only gave him limited info. A short while later he was picking me up at the airport after I landed. We drove straight over to the Wells Fargo arena on the ASU campus where I scalped a ticket outside the arena. Benny and I didn't sit together but made plans to connect after the game.

I didn't tell Benny what was in the duffle bag; I'd brought the money with me because I was planning ahead. I knew in my gut that if Hedake and ASU lost the game and didn't cover the spread against UCLA, that Hedake would be backed into a corner once again and have no choice but to give me the USC game coming up in two days on Saturday. If that happened, I was prepared. I was already on the West coast, with my cash in hand ready to go, an hour's flight away from Vegas.

I sat just six rows off the floor for the game against UCLA that night by myself, with only my duffle load of cash to keep me company. I had it strapped over my shoulder and hugged close into my lap. Being in an arena with over 12,000 people, and this cash on my lap, I couldn't help but have thoughts about how perilous my situation was. Benny probably knew I'd brought some cash with me, just not how much.

What if he was pissed about me shorting him in the stacks I gave him after Game Two? What if he told someone and I got robbed?

I kept thinking that I had two and a half million reasons to be nervous.

I never got robbed, so I was just glad I was able to watch the game and personally see how *true* money, pressure, and fear could motivate a player to be his best. At that point I was just a fan watching an NCAA game. Even though it was one I had a little insight on.

I have to say, that even though ASU was clearly outmatched, it was a *great* game; probably one of the best I'd seen. For most of the game it was either tied or a single basket lead by either one of the teams. Hedake's play was "inspired"; he led the team in points, and you could tell he was doing all he could to fight and will his team to victory. I even found myself rooting for him to win. I mean, everyone loves a come-from-behind underdog, and no one more than me. The twenty thousand was a distant thought to me, and didn't even matter much at that point.

Then with just under a minute to play, UCLA took a two-point lead, ASU missed a shot on their next possession, and UCLA scored again to put UCLA up by four points. Right on the betting line number!

With about six seconds to go, ASU missed another shot and UCLA's "Big George" Zidek rebounded the ball with a little over two seconds left and was fouled by one of the ASU players. This gave Big George two shots on the free-throw line. He made the first one, making it a five-point game.

I remember looking directly at Hedake's face when George made that free throw. He was destroyed, beaten down, and looked flat-out empty.

Then Big George made the second free throw as well, putting UCLA up by six points. The game was over, or at least to everyone involved except Hedake. With two lousy seconds left on the clock, all of the other players, coaches, and spectators knew the game was done.

Now here is the part that will tell you all you ever need to know about sports, sports betting, this adventure, its players, and its gamblers. When Big George made that second free throw, there were two plus meaningless seconds left on the clock and UCLA was up by six points. Another basket by ASU wasn't going to make a difference, but right when that second free-throw went through the basket, from where I sat I heard Hedake *yell* to one of his teammates, "Get me the ball *now!*"

Just picture it. The second free throw is made, UCLA up by six, the coaches from both benches are starting to walk towards half court to shake hands, the other nine players on the court are standing still on the court and starting to give each other the proverbial congratulatory "good game" handshakes. The game was over, right? Nope, not for Hedake it wasn't.

With what I can only call reckless abandon, and *without* any of the other players guarding him or even remotely caring, Hedake got the inbound pass that he'd demanded, did a sprint dribble up the court going about as fast as I've ever seen anyone move, and just as the clock was about to expire, set up behind the three-point arch and launched a three-pointer.

The shot rimmed in and out, leaving the final score at UCLA 76 to ASU 70. ASU lost the game and Hedake failed to cover the four-point spread he needed to win his bet. Now he owed me $22,000 and I'm sure he had *no* idea how he was going to pay it.

I often think about what Hedake's reaction might have been if that shot went in. Would he have shown excitement over winning $20K even though his team just lost the game? That sure would have been interesting.

I will never forget the image of him after he missed that three-pointer. Crunched down on the court on all fours, head hung down in defeat, with no one near him and all the players and coaches walking off to the locker room. I really honed in on that image.

As it turned out, so did the FBI.

After the game I just wanted Benny to handle things and talk with Hedake directly. I didn't want to meet him or for him to know that I was even in town watching the game. I just had Benny take me to the airport and caught a flight from Arizona to Vegas. Once there, I checked into Bally's around Midnight and called up Benny.

"I met with Hedake," he told me, "and he's all set for Saturday's game against USC. He wants another fifty thousand and for you to wipe away the twenty-two grand he just lost as well. What do I tell him?"

I kept it nice and simple.

"We have a deal."

Chapter Nine:

Game Three

I woke up early Friday morning in my Bally's hotel room and called Mangiamele and Vince Basso in Chicago, telling them that were "on" for another game on Saturday night. The two of them jumped on a plane like their pants were on fire and met me in Vegas that afternoon.

That evening I bet some early lines for the Saturday game at a few of the larger hotels; maybe around $80,000 to $100,000 worth, with ASU as a 9½ to 10-point favorite against USC. I bet very carefully as I didn't want to move that betting number or alert anyone to a line movement. After all, it wasn't Super Bowl weekend anymore and eyebrows would be raised with this being the third ASU game in a few weeks taking large amounts of money on it.

Then Saturday morning came and I was ready to pound once again. My cash was ready, and I knew that Mangiamele and Basso had brought theirs as well. Once again I had Benny set me up a brief chat with Hedake on the phone before I started putting my dollars at risk. This time the call was quick and to the point.

"Hedake? Don't win by more than five. Are we clear?" I said…

"Okay. Not a problem."

He seemed confident and based on that conversation, the three of us set out to start betting the game. This was no longer Super

Bowl weekend, so not attracting attention when betting that kind of money on a somewhat meaningless college basketball game was quite the task.

People think of Vegas as this gambling mecca that takes any and all action, but that's not the case. Vegas is a corporate machine that most of the time is scared of big action. They equate big money to smart money. Especially sportsbook action.

Looking back now, I did get a bit sloppy. I just kept betting and betting, doing all I could to beg and convince the books to take my money. In the process people asked questions. I ended up filling out several CTR forms and the betting line kept dropping lower and lower. That was *not* a good thing.

A dropping betting line attracts attention.

I finally did get my $2.5 million bet on USC plus the points, but in the process the line had moved down to 4½ to 5. That was a *same day*, five-point betting line move on a regular college game with no injuries reported. That line movement alone, plus the money I bet, would get the attention of people I didn't want to get noticed by. Even the bookmakers back East were starting to ask me questions when I called in my bets to them.

People were starting to connect the dots. Dots I didn't want connected, especially from the types of people connecting them.

The game was scheduled for late that Saturday and was to be televised, so the three of us watched it in my hotel room at Bally's. Watching the game, right from the opening tip-off, I started to think that the game didn't even *need* to be fixed. ASU came out ugly and just plain flat. USC dominated and led pretty much the entire game. Maybe it was the deflating loss two days earlier against UCLA, maybe it was Hedake and company just exhausted from the roller coaster ride they'd been on, but I will tell you it was a beating.

USC ended up winning the game 68-56, but that score doesn't even really reflect how badly ASU was beaten down that night.

After the game, the three of us went from hotel to hotel cashing tickets. That night felt like a dream. It just seemed like whatever I touched turned to gold.

This time, I ended up collecting about $5.0 million in cash.

Mangiamele and Basso were partying with women and drinks as though they were kings. Not me. I was beat, both physically and mentally. I scheduled a massage appointment at Bally's spa for the next day and crashed in my room while flipping through television stations.

For the first time, my intuition was tingling. I had some bad feelings about how everything was going down; the number of people who knew things, and the people who were asking random questions. Nothing I could put a finger to, just... I almost wish I could call it instinct, but instinct implies something that I would have listened to.

Mangiamele and Basso flew back to Chicago the next day, while I stayed in Vegas and went to my parents' house for a good old-fashioned home-cooked Italian meal. If you want a great little feast, skip the restaurants and get an invite from someone's Italian mother; you won't regret it. I shared what had happened with my Dad and the money I'd made. All he could do was shake his head in disbelief. Even with his limited sports knowledge, he knew how sloppy I'd been.

After successfully explaining to Tony at the CBOT that I was "stuck in Vegas," I flew back to Chicago that Monday.

There came a moment at airport security when I put my large duffel on the conveyer and watched it go through the X-ray machine. On the other side the security guard must have seen some odd looking contents, and opened up the bag to look inside. Then he looked at me.

The look on his face was priceless.

He stared. Did a double take and let his imagination run wild. That was the first moment when it actually hit me about the money I was carrying, and I thought I might get in some trouble for it. But then he zipped the duffel back up, didn't say a word to me, and waved me on, never saying a word.

That is how it was in those pre-9/11 days. I hoisted the duffel to my shoulder—there's nothing quite like feeling the true weight of your winnings (almost a 100 lbs. of it) — and headed to my gate. By the time I was on my flight home I had five million in cash perched on my lap and thought nothing about it.

The in-flight movie was *Rudy*, a football movie about an underdog achieving his dream. I'd never seen it, but man did I love that film. I was entranced in it the bulk of the flight. The plot, the music, the entire film - I guess I connected with the 'no one believes in you' theme behind it. In fact, towards the end of the film when Rudy finally got to play in an actual game for Notre Dame, I actually started to cry.

That was so unlike me. Shedding tears was not anything close to common in my world. I was in such a trance with this film and its story that I was oblivious to focusing on the craziness of the past few days. A few minutes later when I realized that I was crying, I started laughing out loud.

Laughing because it all of a sudden hit me... Here I was, twenty-five-years-old, with five million in cash sitting on my lap that I'd just made fixing a few college basketball games, alone on a public airplane, crying like a baby watching the movie *Rudy*. That entire sequence made me laugh, even to this day.

When I got back home to Chicago, I collected just north of another $300,000 from the bets I made with the bookmakers on the USC game. Once I had that in hand and all my money collected, I paid Hedake and Benny the $50,000 each that I'd committed to. With the money paid out, I felt that this series of events had finally come to its conclusion.

When all was said and done, and all obligations paid, I'd made a little over *five point one million in cash* for fixing three games. Even with that, a part of me thought that I should have done better and made more money because of the information I had, while the other part thought it was a good thing that this was finally over.

As it turns out, it wasn't over. Not by a long shot.

Chapter Ten:

Game Four- The Explosion

I got back to Chicago on February 21, 1994. I wanted to kick back some and put the money I had made to work in the markets. My focus was to learn how to trade, and the ASU dollars I'd made were going to be my springboard. I thought everything was over, and I knew in my heart I had no intention of putting any more energy into another idea like that. But the demons wouldn't let me out of their grasp, and late night on Thursday, March 3, my home phone rang. It was Benny.

"Hey, listen to this, Joe. ASU just lost a home game against Washington State, which means they're probably not going to get selected for the NCAA tourney. What do you think about fixing one more game?"

"Benny, man, I'm out. You weren't straight with me. You know that and so do I. Besides, getting dollars off on the USC game was next to impossible."

"Joe, it's just for *one* more game. The one coming up this Saturday against Washington. You're never gonna get this chance again."

I did try to resist the temptation. I knew the scrutiny that would follow if I went back to Vegas again and tried to bet serious dollars on or against ASU. So, I pushed back one more time.

"Benny, you're not getting it. I'm tired of this. I don't want to do this anymore. Heat is everywhere, and all over me"

"Okay, wait. So this wasn't *exactly* my idea."

Something about his tone didn't sound good, almost like he was frightened, so I asked.

"Benny, what's going on?"

"Well, remember that layoff bookmaking operation I used to lay off your action when I opened a betting account for you?"

"The one I beat down week after week during football season, yes I remember." I replied…

"Well, that operation is owned by a guy that goes by the name of Big Red."

"So, never heard of him. Why should that mean anything for me?"

"He's a big time drug dealer in Arizona, and they *don't* call him 'Big' because he's small and skinny. He weighs like six hundred pounds. He's like a white bloated whale with red hair that walks on land."

"So this Big Red guy found out about the three games we fixed and put pressure on you and Hedake to do another one. Is that what you're telling me now?" I said…

"Hey, I break easy, okay? Anyway, with ASU basically out of the NCAA tourney, we have an opportunity to hit one more game; the one for this Saturday against Washington. ASU is gonna be a big favorite. It's the only one left, Joe. With the season winding down there's nothing else on the schedule that will work. Come on, Joe, just this one more time?"

Sigh.

I didn't want to believe any of this at all. I thought I was out, and had made plans to put my dollars to work in the markets. I knew how hard it was just betting on the USC game, the questions and attention that was on me because of that line move. Doing another one just two weeks later I knew I was asking for trouble. Plus, I knew that with or without me, Benny and Red were doing this game. So, since I was already knee deep at this point, I figured I'd be better off being involved.

I was also young, stupid, and felt bulletproof because I thought I could out-think everyone else. Even though the betting was a struggle, I oddly embraced the challenge. Challenge and all, it still seemed easy. As the cliché goes, greed won and finally got the best of me.

Another way I look back at those days now is that, simply put, I just didn't think at that time what I was doing was so very wrong. I knew it wasn't exactly right, but I guess somehow at that immature age, I viewed various degrees of rights and wrongs. And a no harm, no foul type of thing seemed like an almost acceptable "right".

Because of the gambling world I lived in- i.e., the CBOT- I somehow managed to view this ASU venture as simply going to Vegas to bet on a few games. And selectively chose to overlook the bribery part of the equation. I ignored my intuition and put the final nail in my own coffin. So, my answer?

"Okay, Benny, just *one* more time, then I'm out."

"Oh, you won't regret it, man. When we win this one, remember this conversation. You will owe me down the road."

On a personal note, I was just about to get married. Yeah, I know, where did I ever find the time? I wasn't into the social scene, and at the time a girl I had met during my short college stint seemed like a right choice.

The game to be fixed was that Saturday, March 5, against Washington, and my soon-to-be wife had planned a massive bridal shower for Sunday the sixth. So with me agreeing to do this game, I had to break the news to her that I was going to Vegas on Friday but would be back Sunday morning, bright and early for the shower.

To her credit- and that pains me to say- she urged me not to go. Not because of the bridal shower and the possibility of my being late, but because she had a bad feeling about me doing this entire thing one more time.

I can't say that I wasn't given enough warnings. Maybe if I'd listened to any of them this story would never have to be told.

Still, I convinced myself that I *had* to go, not because of pressure from Benny or any Big Red nonsense. The *real* reason I wanted back in was that I'd convinced myself that:

**Ten million dollars in cash sounded so much better
than five million did.**

So, I lined up everything I needed, got the money from the bank, booked the flight, and flew to Vegas on Friday night, March 4, 1994.

I arrived with my bag of cash. Mangiamele and Vince Basso flew out with me as well, and together we set out that night to start with the early overnight betting lines, just like I did in games two and three. I was holding nothing back.

ASU was a heavy favorite against the much weaker Washington team. The opening line posted ASU as a 12 point favorite. I'd brought five million dollars in cash with me to Vegas for this game, and especially after the "pain" I'd endured betting the USC game, I knew I had to be smart and very careful not to move the betting line in any big ways or let certain people see me with action that had ASU involved in it.

So on Friday night I only bet around a hundred thousand on the overnight lines, and planned to wake up early Saturday morning and pound the casinos with the remaining money I had with me.

Early Saturday morning I started hitting the usual big places first, making my bets on Washington plus the points, and managed to get off about $1.5 million with no issues at all. Around noon it seemed as if the betting line for the game started to drop like a rock. Every sportsbook in Vegas questioned the action. I'd walk up to a betting window and tellers would call over supervisors immediately, and would ask me why I wanted the bet.

Even with these issues, over the next couple of hours I still painfully managed to bet another eight to nine hundred thousand on the game. I was even able to stop along the way to make my calls to the Midwest and East Coast bookmakers and place a little over $300,000 in action on the game with them.

About the same time, I started to hear from several ticket writers, tellers, and supervisors that a group of college-age kids were literally emptying *boxes* of cash to bet on Washington plus the points as well. These kids had *no* idea what they were doing or how to be careful not to move a betting line. They just had a ton of money with them and were betting it all at the windows.

I remember being at the Mirage sportsbook trying to make a bet with one of the tellers. As I was waiting for a supervisor to "approve" the action, the teller leaned over and told me that some 600-pound guy with red hair was just at his window betting the same game. Right then I knew in my gut that this was gonna be a disaster.

At this point I was in for over $2.5 million cash in Vegas and over three hundred thousand or so with the bookmakers. With this cash out and *gone* from my hands, I look up at the betting boards, and saw the line had just dropped to 5.

Most of the bets I had at this time were in the range of Washington plus 12 all the way down to plus 8, both in Vegas and with the book-maker accounts, so I still felt that I was somewhat in a better spot than what was current condition was.

As messed up as I can tell you that I *knew* the situation was, I *still* wanted to bet. I can't explain it, nor can I explain why. But I still had another $2.5 million in cash left on me, on a game I thought I knew the outcome on, and I wanted to bet it. I was focused on my vision to leave Vegas with that preset ten million dollar number.

But now the betting line was at '5' and *still* dropping.

Only one thing I could think of doing at that time, other than pull my hair out, was to call Benny and make sure he knew how pissed I was.

"Benny, what the *hell* is going on? I'm chasing college kids dropping big bets everywhere at every casino and the line is dropping like a rock."

"It's Big Red, Joe. He sent them all over to Vegas to make the bets for him."

"Well, these kids don't have a *clue* as to lines or the ways of betting and they're making a *mess* of things."

"I know, and that really sucks, but Red shook me and Hedake down *hard*. I mean, I gotta tell you that I like my spleen right where it is, and I imagine Hedake likes his legs in their original condition."

"Not what I bought into, Benny. Not what we discussed. You're not gonna be happy with me when this is done."

"Listen Joe, I'm sorry that the line is dropping so hard and that Red's involved, but that guy is one scary dude I can't mess around with!"

Looking back now, when he was telling me all this it became clear to me that Big Red was probably the one who sent the group of kids out to bet the USC game as well. Benny had to be playing both sides and getting paid from both of us. Regardless of Red being big or not, the guy must have been a complete moron to bet the way he was and attract the attention he did.

"Just don't worry about the game, Joe. Hedake won't think twice about getting sideways with Red and will do what we need him to do no matter what the betting line is."

"I don't like this, Benny, not at all… But I guess at this point, I don't have a choice. You put me in a real bad spot." I said…

"All will be good, Joe. No way Hedake is gonna let Red or the Chicago mob down."

Maybe I was desperate at this point, or maybe I just wanted to believe anything because I had three successful games under my belt already, but at the time Benny's story and assurances seemed to make absolute sense to me, so I decided to just press on and finish betting.

The Vegas reality, though, was a much different story. With the line dropping and rumors running around town, it had become next to impossible to bet any more money on this game. Every time I'd walk up to a betting window and even mentioned either ASU or Washington to the tellers, supervisors would be called over and start in with all kinds of questions.

After a lot of this struggling, yelling, and basically fighting for any hotel to take my action, I finally ended up betting around another $300,000 on Washington plus 4.5 to 5 and gave up. I was now in this mess for around $3.1 million and just had a *real* bad feeling about what the outcome was going to be.

I finally walked back to Bally's being pissed at myself for allowing this to happen. I ended the night putting my remaining money in a safe deposit box, and went up to my hotel room alone and just laid down on my bed. I was mentally exhausted and my mind was still racing. Then with about half an hour before tipoff, I had a brainstorm.

The betting line at this point had dropped from ASU minus 12 all the way down to ASU minus 3. That's a 9 point line movement on a college basketball game on the *same* day with *no* injuries. In fact, to this day that is still the largest one-day line movement *ever* on a betting line. Nothing felt right and I felt in my gut that I had a loser on my hands, so I literally jumped out of bed, ran down the halls, took the elevator downstairs, went to the safe deposit box where I took out all my remaining cash, and ran over to the sportsbook to make a bet.

It's now about ten minutes before the start of the game.

I was going to bet on the *other* side.

I actually tried to bet 2 million dollars on ASU to win minus 3. The way I figured it, with all the junk happening with Big Red and the 9 point drop of the line, fix or no fix, I had to go the other way. There were way too many things going against me.

At this point, I only wanted my money back. When you're a trader or gambler, and your goal is to simply get back to even just so you can get back to what you once HAD, you're toast. I can tell you that feeling *sucks!* At that time, that was the feeling I had. I only wanted to unwind the day and get back to even.

Betting on ASU minus 3 for two million when I already had Washington plus 8 all the way to 12 points for three million, seemed like a smart hedge. One that I could live with even if Hedake performed. I did not want to get pounded with a total loss. Plus, it was one hell of a middle to capture both sides if ASU ended up winning the game by 4 to 7 points.

Bally's sportsbook's management actually considered writing this bet for me. The supervisors walked up to me and asked me questions to see if I was flexible on allowing them to write half of the money at ASU minus 3, and the other half at ASU minus 4½. I agreed to that plan, but needed them to hurry because the game was about to start. Right when I agreed to the bet the way they proposed it, Lenny Del Genio walked over to me. He was the race and sportsbook manager at Bally's at the time and was red-faced with anger, pointing his finger at me and yelling at the top of his lungs for all to hear.

"YOU!"

"Huh? What'd I do?"

"I'm not taking any more action from you. You're the reason all this *shit* is happening!" he yelled…

Now, I was young, in good shape, and a somewhat arrogant kid from Chicago who didn't take a lot of crap, so I tossed it right back at him. Loudly, so everyone there knew I wasn't going to be barked at.

"Hey, Del Genio, it's your *job* to take whatever I or anyone else throws you, crap or not! You're supposed to be the sportsbook, so take your panties off, do your job, and write the action."

"I will not take this from you. You're a little punk kid with a few bucks, so go fix your action elsewhere."

"Oh, you'll take it because it's your job and I have the money. Don't blame your pathetic life on me."

What he said after that I don't think can be classified as actual words, but the intent was quite clear. Lots of yelling and finger-pointing, and it looked like he was going to actually physically explode. His ranting became a lot clearer, though, when he called security over to escort me out of the hotel and off the property. By that point the game had started and I was able to see the first few minutes of it on the monitors before being led out.

Washington opened the game tearing ASU apart. I'm not sure what the exact score was when security led me away, but I know in the first couple minutes, Washington had a double-digit lead. That, at least, made me feel somewhat better about my money bet.

As I was led off the property, I kept thinking that maybe Hedake was indeed scared to death. Maybe he didn't care at all anymore and was 100% gonna toss the game away. Maybe he told his teammates about his troubles and they were now behind him too. I tried to stay positive. These thoughts all went through my head as I searched for any kind of hope.

As for my personal well-being and state of mind, I knew that was done. I was physically and mentally spent...

Once security hauled me off the property, I went across the street to the Barbary Coast Hotel and called my parents' friend who ran Bally's: Bill Sullivan. Bill took pity on me and arranged for me to get back in the hotel through a back door so that I could go up to my room with my remaining cash and relax.

The ASU game was on television in the room. I remember wanting to watch the game, but by this point, after my struggles fighting with sportsbook people trying to bet, and the uneasy feeling in the back of my head about the huge amount of money I still had at risk, well, I was beat down. I was just mentally exhausted to a point that sitting on the bed in that room, with the TV on, wasn't enough to keep me awake.

I kept my eyes open until finally right around halftime and seeing a score on the screen showing a tie game, but that was it; the last sight I saw on that game. I closed my eyes and knew in my heart that this was *not* going to turn out well, and with that on my mind I fell asleep.

It was several hours later when I woke. The TV was playing some infomercial. I had no idea of the final score of the game, so I tossed some water on my face and headed downstairs to the sportsbook to see the final score that was posted on the big betting screens. As I was looking at the scoreboards, it felt like all eyes in the room were fixed on me; it was a very odd feeling.

Worse than being stared at was to see the final score: ASU 73 to Washington 55.

The game had gone from Washington being up double digits early in the game when I was booted out of the hotel, to an almost tied game close to halftime, to ASU blowing Washington out of the water by 18! ASU had covered the spread, and *all* the bets I'd made in Vegas and with the bookmakers, and all of the others made on Washington that brought the betting line down to a closing number of three, all of them *LOST!*

Almost FOUR *million* dollars, all gone.

Naturally, there was just one thing to do… That was to try and feel better by passing the blame. I called Benny.

"Benny, you scum-sucking…"

Benny interrupted, "Joe, Big Red's looking for me everywhere, man! He- He wants to pull my liver out through my teeth and cook it with onions. Man, this is not good, not good at all."

"Big Red is only one of your problems. You owe me money now too. I'm not taking this loss telling you its okay and sitting on my hands. Why didn't Hedake handle the score?"

"I think Hedake's ready for a padded room, Joey. You think *I'm* bad? That guy's a complete wreck!"

"Benny, what *happened?*"

"Hedake told me that the feds and the Nevada gaming commission gave the entire team a pep-talk, man. Right there in the ASU player's locker room at halftime."

My heart sank like a stone.

Turns out that the Nevada gaming commission alerted the feds about the "unusual" betting activity for not only the ASU-Washington game, but for a few of the prior ASU games as well. With this, and the way that the ASU team was playing in the first half, Benny told me two FBI agents and a rep from Nevada gaming went into Frieder's ASU team's locker room at halftime. He told me the speech that was given to the team that day went something like this.

"I don't know what you kids have been up to in today's game or a few in the past, but know that in due time we are going to figure it out. In the meantime, we strongly suggest that you kids play up to your abilities in the second half."

The first thing I could think of when I heard Benny tell me about how the FBI and gaming officials were in the locker room at halftime was a voice screaming in my head, "What kind of bad luck do I have?" Hearing about them in that locker room *really* pissed me off.

I had just lost almost four million bucks on a game because the government decided to give the team I bet against a pep talk at half-time. How crazy was *that*?

And yet, I knew, even with or without the pep talk from the feds, I'm pretty sure that even *if* Hedake and the team had performed and tanked the game as I needed, all of the betting tickets in Vegas would have been frozen out and questioned. Since the gaming commission was now involved, any tickets bet would have been investigated when presented. Meaning it was only a matter of time before that vice closed tighter and tighter around who was involved.

I flew back to Chicago early Sunday morning and attended the bridal shower, but everything that day was just a complete blur; the entire prior 48 hours was a complete fog. When I looked back at those bridal shower pictures, I looked like a ghost. In the pics I resemble a bridegroom from hell, who tried to go the distance with Tyson.

This was only the beginning of my beating.

Chapter Eleven:

Investigated

I got married and several months of wedded bliss went by before my doorbell rang on a Saturday. I answered it and came face to face with a pair of badges.

The FBI was at my home.

Not knowing any better back then, I invited them into my home where they began asking me several questions about being in Vegas, why I go there, and my betting activity.

"I go to Vegas because my parents live there," I said. "And, yes, I like to bet."

"You really seemed to like the ASU games," one of them said. "Why is that? Why is it you seem to bet big on their games?"

"I don't know. Seemed like the past few times I've been out there, those games have had the line movements. I follow money and betting line movements to try and stay ahead of the numbers." That was all I could muster up…

"You put out quite a bit of money against ASU on those games," the first asked. "Why so much?"

Again, I was an arrogant kid with a few bucks who actually thought I could out think these two FBI agents.

"Because I can," I shrugged. "I make enough to justify what I do. I like betting from time to time. That's not against the law. I'm sure you guys have seen my tax returns, right? Now if you don't mind, I have a few things to do this afternoon."

It was a pretty short conversation. They knew the position I was taking with them and left with no further questions. I never heard from them again.

Sure, at the time there was a *lot* of speculation swirling around, newspaper stories of rumors with BS facts, all kinds of talk on television and sports radio, but for years *nothing* was concrete and the feds were going nowhere trying to make a case. I was still safe. I thought all was a distant bad memory.

Years went by and the ASU fix, the anxiety and the cash made became a distant memory. Over time, any idea of it resurfacing or any legal trouble seemed to be the furthest thing from my mind.

By 1996, I'd taken a few lumps trading at the CBOT. The Persian Gulf War and the Mexican peso devaluation took some chunks out of my trading account. I decided to leave the CBOT and move to Arizona, where I took a job with a securities firm doing estate planning and asset allocation. It was a fairly simple life and Arizona was a pretty laid back place to live. About the exact opposite of life in Chicago. But, it seemed like the perfect place to raise a family.

By mid-1998, a full four plus years after the last ASU fixed game, I was a father of two beautiful girls and learning to enjoy the quiet suburban life when I get a call from Michael LaPat, my dad's prior business attorney in Chicago. The feds had contacted Michael thinking he was still our family attorney. Michael called my dad in Las Vegas to get my home phone number, and he called me directly.

After some short pleasantries, he launched into it.

"Joe, I took a call from an FBI agent today; you're the subject of a criminal federal investigation."

"Wha- What do you mean?

"The FBI is after you, Joe. I suggest you get a criminal attorney to represent you right away."

"The feds... You got to be kidding me. Any idea what it's about?"

"They said it was about gambling. Criminal is not what I do. Just find someone to handle this ASAP."

Not knowing any better, and thinking I could again out-think whatever BS they could toss my way, I hired two Arizona attorneys by the names of Tom Connelly and Tom Marlowe. At the time, they sold me on their experience, and led me to believe that together, we could beat this.

Looking back now, their real experience was in settling and avoiding. They didn't want or plan to fight the case; their focus was to take fees and plead out as quickly as possible.

Never being exposed to that world, I was extremely naïve with the entire criminal process. Naïve or not, what I did know was that I was indeed guilty of bribing someone. With that knowledge, and knowing I did do wrong, I decided to plead guilty to one count of conspiracy to commit sports bribery, provided the feds agreed not to pursue any charges against my dad and brother.

Once I agreed to plea, it was very eye opening to learn how the government built the case, the resources they had at their disposal, and the crazy - sometimes - flat-out dirty tactics they used to coerce stories from others to fit things as they needed them to be. Early on I argued and actually thought I could beat the case, so I sat down with the government thinking that I would tell them the same lousy stories that I'd told the FBI agents at my home in Chicago four years earlier.

When I got to the Arizona office of the Assistant United States Attorney, it became *very* clear that the story I had used in Chicago wasn't going to work. They had a couple of tables set up in the office piled high with more information about me than I could have remembered about myself.

They had camera footage from various Vegas hotels, room service bills, phone bills, phone records, safe deposit box slips, flight information, pay phone records, home phone records, banking statements, tax returns, interviews from hundreds of people, and the list goes on and on...

These guys hadn't been idle at all; they'd documented every detail of my life, along with my actions for the past five years. They laid it all on the tables for me to see.

I didn't have to be real smart to know this was NOT GOOD...

As time passed and the government was putting together the final pieces of its case, I happened to find out exactly how they were able to break the case open, get my name, and get so many details.

Earlier, I mentioned that my brother's roommate would call me in Chicago asking me for life advice and sports picks because he was getting beat up on his own selections. This was the same guy who read me the betting lines from Benny's operation, and that was how I found out that Benny's lines were so messed up that I started betting and beating Benny week after week. This roommate friend of my brother was named Pete Nassos.

Pete's nickname in college was "make-a-buck Pete". He came from a wealthy family in Chicago; his father was a well-respected surgeon. As it turns out, however, Pete and I both seemed to have looking for shortcuts built into our DNA.

At that time, it had been almost five years since I last saw or heard the name Pete Nassos, so I never knew what Pete was involved in. I had no idea that one of Pete's hustles while going to school at ASU was stealing credit cards, then using those credit cards to buy electronic equipment, such as computers and TVs. Then he'd sell that stuff to students for cash at discounted prices.

In 1997, when the government had basically nothing on their ASU point-shaving case investigation except speculations and rumors, Pete and a guy I'd never met named Brett Wells, I was told were caught outside an electronics store in Tempe, Arizona, using stolen credit cards.

With Pete coming from money, there was no way his doctor father, was going to allow his son to be branded a felon, so Pete and Brett did their best impression of Monte Hall on "Let's Make A Deal," giving the government all the information they both knew on the ASU games. After all, the ASU case had sizzle to it; it was a trophy for any FBI agents and U.S attorneys who could bring it forward. A state university scandal, the integrity of college basketball called into question, nationwide attention—a big score indeed.

The little nuggets of information supplied by Nassos and Wells opened the doors the government needed to secure a case.

Nassos and Wells also directed the feds to Benny's old college roommate, a guy named Barry. I wouldn't have known this guy if he were sitting next to me. But, now, with the feds on him, I learned that Barry got busted outside of Phoenix with a car trunk full of pot.

I'm pretty sure it's safe to say that since Benny and Barry lived together, Barry knew most of the details that went down on the ASU games and that he was going to use any and all of those details to get himself out of his drug troubles. So, he made a deal with the government in exchange for his freedom as well. A deal that would put me square in the crosshairs of the one of the largest sports betting scandals of the century.

None of those guys were ever charged with any of the crimes they were involved with. They *all* walked. They gave the feds everything they knew about ASU on a silver platter, and got immunity for their illegal actions.

The government was able to make its case on the ASU scandal by allowing a drug dealer caught red-handed and a couple of thieves to completely walk free of their own crimes. The ASU case was higher up the criminal food chain. The "catch a bigger fish" concept justified those guys to trade their knowledge in exchange for forgiveness on their own sins. Funny how that works.

There is an image that remains ingrained in my mind the day I went into the Assistant U.S Attorney's office to see what they had against me. They showed me an actual picture.

It was a picture of a dead man lying on a table at the morgue.

He was an exceptionally large guy, easily over five hundred pounds with red hair. I'd never seen the guy before, so when they asked if I knew him I truthfully said, "No," but it was obviously Big Red. I asked if that's who it was, since I'd heard of him, and they confirmed it. Big Red had died a year earlier of a drug overdose. I thought to myself that Big Red got out of this upcoming mess the easy way.

That was the first time I'd ever seen a picture of a dead guy laying on a table. It was not unlike what you would see on TV.

It was worse.

Even though I had never met Big Red, he was a player in my scheme. His death foreshadowed a future living hell that I was now clearly in the middle of. With deals now in place for Nassos, Wells, and Benny's roommate Barry as well as pressure applied to a few others for statements, the feds had what they needed to indict on the ASU case. The day that the indictments were released was the same day I lost my job, my securities license, and my ability to trade in the markets for others.

My fog had whipped itself into a tornado.

The weeks and months following were an emotional and media frenzy. Friends and family from all over found out about my involvement in this deal because Ted Koppel opened up his "Nightline" primetime nightly news show with the story, and a copy of my driver's license picture on the screen over his right shoulder. And, Peter Jennings did a spot on ABC world news.

Armen Kateyian, then from ABC and HBO Real Sports, practically camped out in front of my home for a couple days straight and released several stories and updates along with any "B" camera footage he could collect.

The fix was the lead story on ESPN for a few weeks, and was front page in most if not all newspapers, including those in Chicago, New York, Arizona, and the *Wall Street Journal*.

I personally received several offers to tell and sell my story, including offers from *Newsweek*, *Time*, and *Sports Illustrated* magazines. I was offered a book deal from Random House and a movie offer from ABC.

I turned them all down.

Money wasn't my focus, and I didn't want the exposure. I was too embarrassed. The only thing I gave any thought to accepting was a $75,000 offer from the *National Inquirer*. I just figured that if I took it, the reputation of the Inquirer would somehow cloud the story. But, I turned that down as well.

Side Note: a couple of years later – spoiler alert - Benny, while in prison, ended up selling his very limited view of the story to FOX, which made it into a movie. The movie lacked all kinds of details mainly because all Benny knew was the one-sided relationship he had with Hedake, and a little bit of flare dealing with drugs on campus and Big Red.

The core of the movie focused on drugs, college life as a bookmaker, and Benny's perception of his pressures. Nothing about the inner details of the fix, such as the money bet and made, or how it was financed; Benny didn't know those parts. In my view, the film totally missed the true essence of the story.

I was not, and for the most part still am not, a litigious person. But when I heard about the movie being made, I had my attorneys file a complaint against Fox. We settled, agreeing that I would give some creative input. What I didn't want was for Hollywood to portray me as an "Italian Mobster" from Chicago who put pressure on a poor innocent black college kid athlete, who didn't know any better.

Sure enough, though, after reading the original script, that was exactly the direction they were headed. I was able to change the underlying tone a bit, but Hollywood still managed to put their own twist on the facts.

Gotta love Hollywood. Whatever sells, I guess.

No one indicted went to trial; everyone made plea bargains. You *do not* take the United States Government to trial. The government has a 96% plus conviction rate for a reason. The main reason is, when they want you, they get you. In this case, boil it down to basics, everyone took pleas because the government had far superior resources and creative ways to make their case. (Not to mention everyone was actually guilty) These facts, coupled with the government's masterful methods of rewarding cooperating witnesses to point fingers where needed from other cases, and your goose was cooked.

It was mandatory for me that any plea deal I took included complete immunity for my dad and brother so that no one else in my family would be dragged in. It was my choice to do what I did. My brother had made the introduction to the ASU group. And, my dad may have made some bets for me in Vegas, but I willed the entire concept to completion. Their immunity was very important to me. It was bad enough that my dad would have to see one of his kids in prison; I certainly didn't want anyone else in my family to suffer from the decisions that I had made.

Sentencing for everyone was on June twenty-first of 1999. Because I'd agreed to a plea of conspiracy to commit sports bribery, and because this was my first offense, I was looking at a range of about twelve to fifteen months of federal prison time. I remember being actually surprised that the sentencing guidelines for sports bribery as compared to other similar crimes were not all that high.

I walked into the courtroom that day still naïve about the system. As a first time offender, I was hoping and thinking that probation could still be an option for the judge; or maybe I'd get thirty to sixty days. Oddly, I wasn't really sweating it. I'd taken their plea and had owned up to my involvement. Before the judge handed down his sentence, I was anticipating this chapter being closed, and just looked forward to putting it all finally behind me. My positive expectations of probation quickly evaporated.

Judge Broomfield sentenced me to 15 months in federal prison.

At first it didn't penetrate. Fifteen months? That was over a year! I stood there, frozen not knowing what to do or how to act. I managed to dodge and avoid the press as best as I could in the hallways and outside the building. Always just saying "no comment" to all the nonsense they asked about. I called my folks in the car, and could hear the outright shock in their voices. This was not what we expected.

After sentencing I went home, took off my suit (I hate suits), and laid on the couch. I remember looking at the time on the VCR: 1:14 it said. I dozed off; when I woke, I thought it was hours later, but it was only 1:27. I remember thinking, *if that was only thirteen minutes, how am I going to make it fifteen months?*

Joe Mangiamele, who was with me on all four of the games, and three out of four of them in Vegas, cried like a little child at the sentencing; he'd ratted out anyone he could pre-indictment and got just a three-month prison term.

Burton admitted to being involved in the first two games and only making a few thousand dollars. With that, he received two months in prison with six months of house arrest as his reward.

Hedake Smith owned up to his involvement as well. And, received a year and one day sentence. That sentence in the federal system equated to approximately a ten month prison term.

We all got punished for our crimes. We all got sentenced. And, all of us paid a price in our own way. That day, we all received the label of "convicted felon".

I try to look at it many ways now. Sometimes I look back bothered by the players' light sentences. In my mind, the events started and stopped with their actions. Sure, I waved the money in front of them. Others will even say I forced them to do certain things. Maybe so…

I understand those arguments.

Probably wrongly, I can look at it the other way. I boil it down to basics again, I wasn't on the court. I wasn't the one missing shots, or the one playing no defense.

As much as I think there was an inequality in the sentences, I knew that for my actions, I was indeed guilty and I needed to be held accountable.

Of the defendants physically present at my sentencing, Vince Basso got hit the hardest, with eighteen months. The government pushed hardest for him because they wanted Vince to tell them *anything* he could about his father's alleged illegal actions, his relationship with Pete Rose, or any info about organized crime. But Vince would not.

The government flew in an organized crime expert, Corbin Weiss, all the way from Washington to convince the judge that Vince was mob material. They said even though Vince was only involved in two of the games - one of which lost - he was still a really bad guy. But Vince stood strong; compared to how things went down on that case, Vince didn't deserve eighteen months. He was the smallest part of what happened.

That's how the government wanted to package it. Because we all know that the words "Organized Crime" and "Mob" can bring a lot of sizzle and sexiness to the headlines, and the strategic use of those words in court by the feds can really nail you to the wall. The eighteen months Vince got provided more luster to the case because of the underworld scare factor.

Benny- Oh, Benny. Everyone ganged up on him, and the government viewed him as the ringleader of the operation, so he earned a whopping 46 months. Now, being ringleader alone based solely on sports bribery laws wouldn't have earned him that long of a sentence, but somehow Benny was tied to a drug charge as well, and that's what got him all that extra time.

I heard that the drug charges were tied to the deal the feds made with his old roommate Barry, and that the drug case angle broke many things open for the feds.

The criminal system is based on capturing the bigger fish. So, in most cases, provided it's more appealing to the government, the concept rewards the small-time guys and allows them to walk. Right, wrong, or indifferent, it's not for me to judge. But, I will state that's our criminal justice system in a nutshell.

At the end of the day, after attorneys' fees and paying off Benny and Hedake, I managed to net a little over one and a half million dollars on the ASU fix. So maybe you think crime pays, but that money wasn't nearly enough to justify being called a "convicted felon" for the rest of my life.

Over time, I slowly learned to accept the 15-month punishment because I finally managed to shake myself and understand no matter how I tried to internally justify my actions, what I did wasn't right. I learned that it had never really been a grey area at all, in fact; there is *only* right and there is *only* wrong, and what I did was flat out wrong. It took me awhile, but time has a way of clarifying things.

Still to this day I struggle with right, wrong, temptation, and grey, just as I did then. At the time all this was going on I wrongly looked at what I was doing as simply going to Vegas and betting on things I just happened to know the outcome to. I certainly knew right from wrong, and was raised in a household where those values were taught correctly.

However, somehow I managed to justify my actions because I thought that I wasn't robbing, cheating, or stealing from anyone personally...it was a nameless, faceless system that lost. I just chose to make excuses when I really knew better.

I was arrogant, young, and stupid; simple as that.

Chapter Twelve:

Building Shammy Man

Now with a felony rap sheet and fifteen months of prison ahead for me, I knew I had few work options available to me. I knew that I needed to start a business and would now have to work for myself.

When it's said that the wheels of justice grind slowly, that's no exaggeration. Between the time I was indicted, pled guilty, and was sentenced, I had a couple years to plan a path.

Not that I think I could have beaten the government's case against me, but I'm sure that I could have secured a better outcome if I'd chosen better attorneys. About the only good thing those two did was introduce me to a man they were also representing on a federal bid rigging case. His name was George Leckie, and he was the Governor of Arizona's chief of staff.

George and I were both sometimes forced to be at the attorney's office for hours on end, so on downtimes we would go downstairs to Morton's Steakhouse for hours and hours to talk. With the felony now in place, and prison in my future, I'd lost my career in the markets and knew I'd need to earn a living once I was free again. I thought that owning full-service car washes would be a great business model; one where the label of 'felon' wouldn't be used against me.

TOSCO is a publically traded company that owns the Circle K gas stations on the west Coast, and George knew its CEO pretty well. At that time, TOSCO had just purchased all of the Arizona EXXON locations, including one on a corner in Scottsdale that I *really* liked. So, I asked George for a favor.

He called his friend at TOSCO and a couple days later I was able to buy the northeast corner of Hayden and Thomas Roads in Scottsdale for $425,000. The next week I had it appraised for almost $800,000. A real steal! Then George used his political weight with Scottsdale to have the site re-zoned so that I could build a brand new full-service car wash on the property. He did all of this for me while dealing with his own criminal case, the media scrutiny around him, and, above all, cancer.

All that time we talked he'd never told me about the cancer. I knew he was frail, but I assumed it was stress related to his case. When I finally built and opened my new carwash, George had passed away. I still to this day keep a stack of business cards I've collected, and George's card still sits atop the pile.

In late 1998 I opened the first of what would be many Shammy Man Car Washes. It cost me a total of about $2.4 million to complete, and because I was a felon waiting to go away to prison, the path of least resistance was to secure financing for the project through the Small Business Administration (SBA), with my Dad and sister signing the loan. The place turned out *beautifully*, complete with my own second floor office that I decked out in a way that allowed me to entertain thoughts of day trading once again.

It was the right place at the right time; Shammy Man did crazy business at that location from Day One. By now you know that I have a problem with doing anything small, and because business was doing so well, I wanted to grow and brand the Shammy Man business model into multiple locations. So in early 1999, while still under indictment waiting to go to prison, I opened up a second location on the west side of Phoenix.

Business was exploding. I had about seventy employees, two SBA loans in place, and I wasn't even in prison yet. I knew I was onto something good with Shammy Man from the start, but first I had to get a fifteen-month prison sentence out of the way.

I was ordered to self-surrender to a federal prison on January 3, 2000. Somehow I'd managed to convince myself that the Y2K computer problem that everyone was talking about would wipe out the computers inside the Bureau of Prisons so that no one would then need me to report, or even miss that I wasn't there.

We all know how wrong *that* line of thinking was.

The morning I went to prison I woke early and said goodbye to my kids. They were only four and five at the time, and it was four in the morning; they were asleep in their beds and I doubt that by breakfast they even remembered that goodbye. But I needed to do it, for me.

Fifteen months, I thought again. Fifteen months. Then I was gone. Subsequently, whenever they asked, my wife told them I was "working."

I surrendered myself on time to the federal prison at Nellis Air Force Base in Las Vegas, Nevada; irony at its best I suppose. Vegas was the place of my crime, and I could see the twinkling lights while sitting in the prison each night — this had to be God's way of making me think.

Surrendering into a prison system the first day makes memories you will never forget, as any first true prison experience isn't complete until you get the cavity search. Just a lovely day, one I'll always remember.

Cavity searches aside, though, I can't really complain too much about my stay at Nellis. As long as you stayed out of trouble, time passed pretty quickly. I do remember my first night there, though. I woke up around three in the morning to use the restrooms, and as I was standing there half-asleep at the urinal, I heard some odd noises behind me. So I turned to look. All I could see were four feet showing from the bottom of a bathroom stall door, with *all four feet* facing the same direction. That was enough to make me sick, and is still a sick Kodak moment that I cannot un-see.

Oh, there are a lot of other crazy Nellis prison stories that could be told. The many fights that would break out in the yard. And, one guy getting sliced from ear to ear with a razor, falling at my feet, simply because he'd looked at some other guy's girlfriend once in the visiting room.

Then there's are the prison hustles; what guys would steal, smuggle in, or what they'd make out of the oddest things would make you laugh. Works of art (really) out of milk cartons, or microwave-prepared pasta that was some of the best pasta I've ever had (and remember, my Italian mother can cook). As for smuggling, well, there were Air Force airmen all over, young guys who were happy to make an extra buck. Most anything you wanted, you could most likely get.

I tried to stay away from all that trouble and just focus on my family and upcoming business ventures. I played a lot of prison softball during my stay; if you think it's bad getting heckled for a bad play by a bunch of guys at a park league on the streets, imagine getting ripped apart by hundreds of inmates in the yard on the prison softball field. Girlfriends, wives, and mothers were usually the targets of these comments, and more than once this kind of verbal abuse brought guys to blows.

There were a few good guys locked up there as well, and many with a *lot* of talent. There was one guy from Guam doing 20 years for drugs who was an incredible artist. I managed to buy a twelve-foot long oil canvas painting of an underwater scene from him. I watched him start it from the first day; it took him four months to complete, and when it was finished I bought it from him for $8000. Later, when I shipped it home to get framed, I was offered $30,000, but no way would I ever sell it. Just far too many memories associated with it. Every time I look at it I remember this guy, the amazing talent, and my experiences while locked up.

My main associates at Nellis were six other businessmen, four of whom were Italian-American and in their early forties to fifties. We'd eat together, walk the yard every night, and talk.

Then there was Russell Pike; he was a tech guy doing fifty months for tax fraud. He had a vision of building a website search engine and calling it "Best Search". He sold me and the others in my little clique on the concept, and combined we all ended up putting in a little more than two million dollars, with me personally donating around $400,000. Best Search never amounted to anything, and who really knows how the money was spent. Yet, I'm still amazed now how he'd actually managed to convince us that we were building a company while locked up in federal prison. But we were dreamers, (maybe more so when locked up) and it made time pass quickly, so in my warped little mind, it was $400,000 well spent.

Pike, by the way, went on to invent the sports drink Xenergy; then, in 2009, he got hit with another tax fraud case and was again sentenced to more than four years in federal prison again. I guess rehabilitation is not for everyone.

Of course, being in prison with a few bucks can get you a few comforts to make your time easier, such as getting your bed made daily, laundry done, better food to eat, and the Las Vegas Review Journal delivered to your bunk every day. As luck would have it, the sports section had an almost daily 5x7 advertisement for a basketball team called the Las Vegas Silver Bullets.

The Silver Bullets played in the International Basketball League, or IBL. The IBL was the minor leagues for the NBA. As crazy as this sounds, Isaac Burton, yes the same Isaac Burton that was sentenced with me for the ASU scandal was the Silver Bullets' star player. That meant that just about every day for the first four or five months of my sentence I got to see a 5x7 ad in the paper for the Silver Bullets with a picture of Isaac Burton dribbling a ball, captioned with something like "IBL player of the week".

Every time I saw that ad, it really bothered me that he was somehow playing basketball while "paying his debt to society." I don't know how or why the courts allowed this but I just bit my lip and kept quiet. I had to keep my focus on getting home.

About six months into my sentence the Sunday edition of the Las Vegas newspaper had a cover story about Isaac Burton. His sentence, for the ASU scandal, had been two months in prison and six months of home detention, but because he was playing basketball and had to earn a living, the government allowed him to serve his sentence at a halfway house in Vegas. The terms of his halfway house stay was that on game nights he got to stay out all night, then on days when the team only had practice, he was allowed to leave at 7AM but had to be back at the halfway house by 7PM. That was how he was serving his "debt to society".

The cover story in that Sundays paper was about two pages long, complete with pictures of Burton, along with interview questions. In one of his answers, he actually said,

"If I had the chance to do it all over again, I would. The money I made was just too hard to pass up."

This guy even had the gall to complain about the halfway house, saying that it was too noisy and that he couldn't get his proper rest.

I flat out saw *red!* Here I was, sitting in a federal prison paying *my* debt to society, while I had two kids at home without their father, two government SBA loans in place, and a *ton* of personal taxes to pay, while Burton was complaining about his special treatment. I thought. how *dare* he bitch and complain about being able to serve his debt to society while still being allowed to earn a living playing professional basketball.

I was pissed! And I wanted everyone to know about it.

Burton's comments just made my blood boil. His quote saying, "If I had a chance to do it all over again, I would," was a slap in my face, as well as a slap in the face of sentencing Judge Robert C. Broomfield. It was BS and I was going to let the world and Judge Broomfield know about it.

I decided to spend a few days in the Nellis prison law library, working on an old typewriter, to type up a four-page letter to the sentencing Judge Broomfield. In that letter I told the judge how hypocritical the sentences were, and that in this case the "debts" being paid to society versus the benefits given were completely out of balance.

In my letter I made several strong points referencing lessons learned on my part, and compared them to Burton's comments about "doing it again if given the chance" as proof that obviously he had learned nothing. Yet here he was, essentially free and able to earn a living, while I sat around locked up.

After I'd completed my letter, I used all of my month's commissary money to buy dimes for the copier machines and stamps for envelopes. I made sixty copies of my letter and sixty copies of the Burton newspaper article, then on each copy of the article highlighted in yellow the comments that Burton made. With copies in place, my plan was to mail the letter and accompanying article directly to the Judge's personal chambers *each day* until I got a response.

I have never been accused of being lazy once I have a plan in mind.

Then four weeks into my mailing campaign, the loud speaker in the prison yard made an announcement.

"Gagliano, report to R and D."

R&D is prison lingo for Receiving and Discharge, so off I went. I walked into a room that had my prison counselor in it, the warden of the whole prison complex, and one of the guards. On the desk was a telephone, from which first came the voice of one of my attorneys.

"Joe, how are you doing?" he asked.

"I'm hanging in there."

"Good. I'm here with Mike Morrissey. You remember him?"

How could I forget?

Mike was the U.S. attorney who indicted me; he was the reason I was in prison. Still, I thought he was a good man who had treated me pretty fairly during the whole process.

"Joe," Mike then broke in, "we have a problem. You're sending letters from a federal prison to a federal judge's chambers. That *can't* happen."

"But Mike," I protested, "I just wanted him to know that-"

"But *nothing* Joe. You can't do that and you need to stop it. Do I make myself clear?"

"Yep, I hear ya', Mike," I sighed.

They hung up the phone and I left the room. When I left the room, I sensed I'd hit a nerve and was on to something they weren't telling me. I felt I was getting their attention and making my point. So, being the glutton for punishment that I am, from that day forward I mailed the exact *same* letter to the *same* judge, not once but *twice* a day.

Fast-forward two more weeks. I've been mailing the same letter and article to the same judge twice a day even after being told by the Assistant United States Attorney *not* to, when over the speakers comes that same announcement once again.

"Gagliano, report to R and D."

I walk into the office and see the same people; counselor, warden, and prison guard in the room. And on the desk is that speaker phone with the same two voices coming out.

"Joe," my attorney's voice begins, "didn't Mike and I tell you a couple of weeks ago not to send anymore letters to the judge?"

"Yes."

"Then why are you still doing it?"

"I just wanted him to know what his sentence did, what purpose it served, and how one guy is making a complete mockery of it while I have to sit here in prison away from my kids."

"Well, now we have a problem," my attorney sighed. "The judge's assistant has called our offices today and ordered an emergency sealed hearing, tomorrow morning in his courtroom at nine A.M."

"And what's going to happen?" I asked…

"Anything the judge wants to happen, Joe. He can give you more time, take away your good time, or ship you to a different prison just to make your life hell. We told you not to mail any more letters, but you did anyway. You really messed up, Joe."

I felt like I certainly did. *Big* time, in fact. After the call we set up a plan where my attorney would call my dad after the hearing so I could get the news directly from my dad as to what happened. All I had to do until then was wait out the night.

I was a complete wreck.

Uncertainty in life is the cause of all stress and anxiety, and on this night I felt I might have pushed the envelope too far. Who knew what they were going to do to me? I could have used some company, but there was no one to talk to. My mom used to always tell me to "let go and give it to God." Maybe for this reason I found myself in unknown territory, reading the Bible, and honed in on Job 11:10. *"If they convene a court, who can oppose Him?"*

I had no idea what was going to happen and thought for sure that I'd pushed the envelope too far this time. Oddly still, I was at peace with my decision and the point I was trying to make in the spirit of balanced scales. Head held high, and all that.

The next day, with my nerves all jangled up, I managed to reach my Dad around 10:30 in the morning.

"So, Dad, what happened?"

"I… I just hung up with your attorney, Joey…"

I could hear it in his voice; something had happened. Something big.

"Dad, what happened?"

"The Judge… Judge Bloomfield, he… Joey, the Judge ordered you to be *released today ASAP!* You're to serve the remaining five months under house arrest. Joey, you're *free.*"

I was in complete shock. I'd already done nine and a half months, but now... Free? I guess my letters really did make a point with the judge. Maybe he wanted to balance the scales and allow me some of the same leeway as he'd given Burton. Maybe he wanted simply to allow me to earn a living for my family while paying my debt to society (and not costing the prison system any more money). Or, maybe he was just tired of getting mail from me. Who knows? Whatever the reason, I was out of prison a couple hours later...

For many years after that day I'd send holiday cards and family pictures to Judge Bloomfield. I guess I wanted him to know that I was still around and that the "system" hadn't beaten me.

Not exactly a clear way of thinking on my part, but the stigma I had within me about being a convicted felon, along with the Catholic guilt I'd been brought up with, always pushed me to show people that I could rise above any situation and accomplish things people doubted I could do.

You know, that just might be as much a weakness as a strength.

Chapter Thirteen:

Riding High

I got out of prison in September of 2000, tired, exhausted, and utterly beaten down. Beaten down from five years of a federal investigation, beaten down from battling a federal indictment, and beaten down from the intense media scrutiny surrounding the case. I was flat-out tired from the stress of being in prison. The only thing I wanted to do was try to relax a bit, make some changes in my life, and get a new start.

I just wanted a break.

My new-found stigma from the label of convicted felon made me feel I was constantly being judged and held to a higher standard than others. I was unsure who I was, what I was supposed to be, whom I could trust, and count on in my life. This uncertainty set me up for another round of bad choices.

I had received an unsolicited offer from a publically traded company to purchase the Shammy Man Car Wash site I owned on the west side of Phoenix. I was into that location for about $900,000 just twenty-four months prior, and now I was being offered almost *three million dollars*, with a quick close.

It was too good to pass up so I took the offer and sold the site rather than continuing to build a solid, strong company on my own, one that would continue to grow into a strong metro Phoenix brand with multiple sites.

I guess other operators must have thought this was a sign that I was getting out of the car wash business, because soon after the west side site was sold, other car wash owners in town made me offers for my Scottsdale site; five offers in all came in.

I ended up selling the Scottsdale location for north of three million in March of 2001 to a great guy who owned three car wash sites in the Phoenix area. His other sites had been struggling and in the red most of the time, so his thinking was to buy my Scottsdale site in hopes of offsetting his overall losses.

After that sale, I was officially out of the car wash business. Now with the ASU criminal case behind me and money in the bank, the stresses in my life evaporated completely. I had a fresh start, and invested a chunk of my new money as a passive investor in some nightclubs in town, and a few entrepreneurial deals here and there. Life was simple.

As it turned out, "simple" is not for me.

After six months of the "simple" life, the guy I'd sold the Scottsdale car wash to called me up to tell me that sales for the site were down by over forty percent. With his other three sites already bleeding money and the Scottsdale site now down as well, he knew that something was wrong. So I worked out a deal whereby I would consult on all four sites for a thirty-day period in an attempt to figure out where the problems were and get him back on track.

A week into my consultation period, I'd learned that while all of his sites were washing a lot of cars, his trusted management team was just robbing him blind, mainly skimming cash by not reporting washes or gift card sales. So I sat him down and told him straight up; the only way he was going to fix the problem was to fire most of his management team.

Unfortunately, he was far too nice a guy to consider that. He was old school, and refused to believe that the same people who were nice to him were the same ones stealing from him. Instead, he gave up, said the car wash business wasn't for him, and decided to sell all four of his locations, real estate and all, to me for a little over $12 million.

It was a *great* deal and put me back in the car wash business once again.

I closed the deal in October of 2001. The first thing I did was give all of them a massive remodel, with new equipment, floors, paint, signage, and so on. I wanted *all* of them to be fully branded Shammy Man sites, and for all of them to supply the same customer experience. I was a businessman again, only this time with a ton of daily revenue and over 200 employees.

For the rest of 2001 and 2002 I bought a few more car washes, extending Shammy Man to a total of eight full-service locations, mostly in the east valley of the Phoenix metro area. We had monthly membership programs and an extreme emphasis on quality. As a result, we owned a fair share of the Phoenix full-service car wash market.

I also hired a lot of upper management. Convenient store managers, oil and lube managers, car wash managers, window tint managers, detail mangers, and so on. I was certainly top-heavy, but I *hated* operations and adhered to a motivation-by-compensation plan that held everyone accountable. To top it all off, I even hired a Director of Operations: my cousin, Joe Scarzone. He was five years younger than me and I trusted Joey in all things, both business and personal. I knew Joey was weak when adversity or pressures arose, so I tried to keep his load simple and focused. For the most part, we got along very well.

The cash flow from 2001 through 2003 was epic. I kept my personal office at the Scottsdale location, where there was so much profit and cash floating around that I made it a point to basically "steal" the first thousand dollars in cash each day from that site, then when deposits from the other sites were delivered I would steal cash from those as well.

Looking back on this now, I wish I'd properly accounted for it all. I wanted to do the right thing. But I still had that trader/gambler mentality in me, from back in my Chicago days. And this mentality felt a little off the top was acceptable. Change is harder than it looks.

I still believed in grey areas.

Even with the cash I was skimming off the top, the company was still tremendously profitable, and gave me the life I *thought* I'd always wanted.

For the first time in my life, I was making money—a lot of money—the right way. But this didn't make me smart-probably the opposite. I spent money on things just because I thought they sounded good. Rather than staying under the radar and saving what I could, I managed to buy a bunch of race horses at the Del Mar track and raced them in the southern California circuit. I bought a sixty-foot boat- I always thought the word "yacht" sounded too pretentious- that I docked at the Marriott Marina in San Diego. I built a 10,000 square-foot home in Scottsdale, and bought a nine-passenger jet from Paul Fleming, owner of Fleming's Steakhouse and PF Chang's. My thinking was so warped that I justified buying the plane so I could get to my boat faster, and just chose to overlook the plane's annual expenses that exceeded $400,000.

The thing was, I never *really* enjoyed any of the toys or perks. I wrongly held on to thinking that because of the felony stigma, I needed to show others their versions of success. In my mind, that meant letting others know I was making money. The toys only seemed to serve my ego and ignorance.

I had three or four cars in the garage at all times. I would buy a new car every time an annual license plate tag had to be renewed. I bought cars for my parents. Gave money to my family members, and put them on the payroll. Health insurance was paid for anyone I thought needed it, paid vacations were given to family and friends, and I never ate at a table where anyone else paid the tab.

To say that I was living in excess would be polite. Oh, there were never the typical "excesses" people think of via sex and drugs; that just wasn't me. *My* excesses were focused on spending, thinking I had to "impress" others. I certainly was *not* a good steward for my new-found blessings.

I can't even count the number of bank wires I'd ask Kerri in my office to make to the Bellagio hotel in Las Vegas. Some nights I would simply be bored and tell the pilots to take me to Vegas, then the next morning wake up and have Kerri wire me one or two hundred thousand so I could gamble. It may sound sexy and fun, but, in hindsight, I don't think I ever really enjoyed any of it.

It's weird how people always seem to want what they don't have, then once they get it, realize that it isn't all that great after all. I guess the grass really *isn't* always greener.

The felon label always followed me, as did the guilt. Even with the Shammy Man Car Wash business exploding and all of the good things we tried to do. And the many charitable donations I made, I couldn't shake the past. Every time Shammy Man was mentioned in an article or news segment I would be brought up as the felonious owner who had gone away to prison for masterminding the infamous ASU point shaving scandal.

You have no idea how much that always bugged me! It never mattered how much good I was doing; the specter of my past always came back to haunt me. When would it end? When was my past mistake going to stop persecuting my reputation?

The answer, I came to realize, was *never.* This label was glued to my back for the rest of my life.

But, I so badly wanted to prove people wrong; to show them that I was past the label of "felon" and doing *amazingly positive* things. Because of this guilt, and because of my desire to be rid of this label of felon, I once again made a poor life choice.

Chapter Fourteen:

Partners with the Devil

One day I received a call from a guy named John Mistler. John and a friend of his, David Beckham, had an opportunity to purchase a defaulted loan for a nice car wash location. Mistler, and ex-football player, the voice of the Arizona Cardinals, and president of a small Arizona bank. And, David the ex-president of a large company called Westcor. Both of these guys had strong business stature. When we met in my office, they told me they could purchase the defaulted loan, before the trustee sale, but only if I had the money in hand right away.

It was a monster site, with a 24-hour convenient store and eighteen gas pumps.

I loved the spot and knew I could make it shine, but because of all the expensive toys I'd wasted money on, I didn't have the $3.3 million in liquid cash on hand to make it happen. Mistler spoke first.

"I'll take you to someone that can help you do the deal," he said.

Mistler was president of the Bank of the Southwest. The majority shareholder was a guy named Reggie Fowler. Fowler and Mistler grew up together in Tucson and played high school football together. Fowler tried to play football after college but never made it. He then worked for Mobile Oil and allegedly stole the rights to a Styrofoam packaging process from them that he was able to successfully market for various uses.

Mistler introduced me directly to Fowler and the two of us hit it off right at the start. Both of us were workaholics, both of us had a passion to build businesses, and we both loved sports.

We worked out a deal that had him putting up the $3.3 million needed to buy the car wash, while I agreed to lease it back from him with a purchase option to buy. Before he did the deal he made one request: he wanted me to move all of the Shammy Man banking business to his bank.

I agreed and the deal was struck.

We bought the site and the following week I took possession. Because this was my first experience with fuel, I soon learned that all of the gas pumping systems and point of sale (POS) systems at the site needed to be replaced. The site had previously been operated as an AM/PM brand store, which meant that all parts were proprietary to AM/PM. The bottom line: if I wanted to actually operate the site, with gas, I would have to spend over $500,000 cash on new equipment. That was 500 grand on a site I didn't own (Fowler did), just so I could get the place to pump gas and to look and feel like the other Shammy Man sites.

I didn't know Fowler all that well, but I figured that, worse case, if he flaked out on me, I had a buyout option on the site. However, Fowler and I did develop a relationship, enough so that I actually thought this guy was my friend. I told him about the ASU matter and my prison time on the first day we met, though I think he already knew. But by me telling him, I'm sure that showed him my transparency.

We traveled together many times to visit various businesses. We both had a passion for aviation. He was a pilot so we would often take his King Air plane to his offices in Denver, or sometimes just fly overnight to Vegas.

Sometimes, after a busy weekend, I'd personally take the cash deposits to the bank for Shammy Man. Fowler would be there and we'd talk, sometimes for hours.

Still, I felt there was something not right about him. He had no real friends, never went out, and I had heard stories about how he'd conducted himself in various business deals and the people he screwed over. But I figured, who was I to judge? After all, I was the convicted felon. Right?

On one of our trips flying back in his plane from Denver he was piloting, and I was sitting to his right. The week earlier there had been an article in the Arizona paper praising Shammy Man for keeping the gas prices the lowest in the east valley. As usual, in that same breath, the article then proceeded to rip me apart for the ASU point shaving scandal. Anyway, we started talking about the article. It was, I truly thought at the time, an in-depth conversation with a friend who really cared.

In that conversation I told him how it bothered me that I couldn't escape my past mistakes, and that the only way I could see overcoming that criminal label was to build a truly *monster* company and do amazing things with it.

I know I probably could have done it myself, and grown the company without excessive debt by reinvesting the profits back into the business with a well-thought-out plan. But, that would have taken time. I was on a mission; I was out to prove people wrong about me, as quickly as possible.

History in my mind repeated itself. I was making the same mistakes that I had before: only this time in a different arena. I wanted it all now!

So Fowler replied to me.

"You find the sites Joe. I'll be the bank and we'll make the deals happen. I know you can operate them, I'll only act as your silent capital partner."

It sounded *perfect!* The answer to my problems.

However, when I brought this concept to my attorneys and accountants (I had good ones then), both said, "He will eat you alive." Did I listen?

113

Nope.

Of course not; I knew better than everyone. Never mind that they knew that Fowler had a reputation for unethical, slimy business activity. I overlooked that and thought, Fowler and I traveled together. We spent time together. This guy was my friend. Right? Even though he was less than ethical with others, there was no way he would ever do that to me.

You see where this is going, right?

With Fowler as my bank, I set my sights on acquiring two monster locations in the east valley. These sites each had about 70 employees, gas pumps, 24 hour C-stores, oil lube centers, detail shops, and so on. I'd worked out a deal with the ownership group to buy both of them for approximately $12 million. Fowler agreed to a deal structure.

He would own the real estate and I would lease them back from him with purchase options to buy when I wanted to. In addition to being the landlord on the real estate, Fowler wanted to be involved in ownership of the overall operating company as well.

I gave Fowler a twenty percent managing interest in the operating company. Justifying his stake in my mind because he'd agreed to provide the operating company with a $1.5 million line of credit. I considered that line of credit vital because of how fast we were growing; we needed the reserves and I knew we didn't have enough.

But the absolute worst part of the deal was in addition to him buying the two new sites, I also allowed him to purchase the underlying real estate from me on four of the other key sites I owned as well. It put a couple million bucks in my pocket, but in the process allowed him to own the real estate on a total of six of the main Shammy Man sites.

All this, *and* he was our acting bank as well. I knew his history, and had been warned by others, but I still put most of my eggs in his basket, believing that we were more than business associates...we were friends.

We completed the two new site acquisitions in June of 2004. From June of 2004 to January 2005, with all sites now operating in full swing, daily revenues were off the chart. Knowing that I had that $1.5 million credit line for rainy days, I decided to reinvest *all* that new money back into the sites for remodeling and branding, with strong focus on the two newly-acquired ones. You see, I had a vision; I wanted *all* of the Shammy Man sites to be consistent with one another, each offering the same customer experience.

Over the course of that seven-month period I spent over $1.5 million on remodeling, getting new equipment and POS systems so that all monthly memberships would be honored at all Shammy man sites. A grand plan indeed, one that used all my operating liquid cash to complete, but in my mind it would be worth it if I could erase a certain label in other people's minds. I *had to* do it right. I had a capital partner in place as my bank, one who'd signed off on a $1.5 million line of credit for rainy day emergencies. What could possibly go wrong?

Never voice that question, for fate *will* give you an answer.

In this case it was the perfect storm (translation=nightmare) for the car wash business. In January 2005 it rained for one entire week straight, and for 25 of February's 28 days it rained as well. Remember, this is *Arizona;* it's supposed to be the desert. On top of that, the forecast called for rain in the first couple of weeks in March. Even the three days in February when it actually didn't rain, it certainly looked like it would.

With all of the company's cash flow of the past seven months reinvested for improvements meant to wow the public, the mortgages, rents, payrolls, and monthly bills for the month of March were now in financial jeopardy.

Not wanting to be late on payments, the last week of February 2005 I put a draw request into Fowler's office for a $300,000 advance on that line of credit. I sent it to Fowler's CFO, since Fowler was in Minnesota trying to buy the Minnesota Vikings. He'd already scheduled the press conference to announce the deal.

He called me around eight in the evening Arizona time, and I remember the conversation like it was yesterday.

"Joe, I heard you put in a draw request to my office for money."

"Yes, I did. Between the rainy weather the past five weeks and the remodeling on the sites of the past seven months, we're running a bit tight." I said.

"What do you need the money for?"

"Just to pay off some of the March rents we owe to you."

"Then I'll handle that internally in my office," he replied.

"Right now my focus is on buying the Vikings. NFL auditors are all over me, so I need to keep my cash in place. But don't worry about it. You're my buddy, I'm not built like that; I got you covered."

I've got you covered. That's what he said. Word for word.

Based on that phone call, I didn't think twice about the March rent shortfall. I paid him on a few of the sites in full, paid all of the other company bills as needed, and left about a $300,000 shortfall on the rents to his office, as I told him I would.

The March rents were due on the first and considered late on the fifth day of each month. Sure enough, at 5:01pm on the 5th I received a default notice from his CFO at his office, as well as an official demand letter from the law firm that had represented my company for years which Fowler had now hired to do some work for him directly. Yeah... along the way Fowler had convinced me to sign a conflict waiver with my attorneys so that he could use the firm as well.

Now I was sitting with a default notice for rents due, and a demand letter from attorneys that had represented me for several years. I was furious, and called him up to tell him so.

"What the hell is this BS?" I screamed.

"I'm sorry, Joe. My office was just doing their job. I wasn't even aware that the notices had been sent to you."

"Then you're going to fix it, right?"

"Of course. Again, I'm real sorry, but the Viking deal had me busy and out of the loop. I'll fix it, really I will."

He must have apologized at least a dozen times during that call. Even so, hanging up the phone that day I was pretty sure what his goal was.

I felt his intent was to hurt me by leveraging details learned from our implied friendship. I also knew at that point I would *not* be able to count on his $1.5 million line of credit, so with all that in mind I paid the March rent shortfall of rents with my own personal money on March 7th, and covered all the other bills needed inside the company so that I could properly focus on a plan that would get Fowler out of my life.

Now, this was about the same time that the press started ripping Fowler apart. The NFL claimed all kinds of fraud with regard to his financial dealings and his net worth; it questioned practically every detail regarding his biography and what he'd claimed to have accomplished. Newspapers and networks kept running stories about all of the various business lawsuits in which Fowler was involved, as well as the many people Fowler had screwed at one time or another. And then there was my involvement with him. The press was having a field day with that.

Imagine it, me a convicted felon for sports bribery, and my partner Fowler trying to buy an NFL team. What kind of luck was this? What are the odds of a business partner I connected with attempting to buy an NFL team? Crazy...

Even worse, all of it was magnified because Fowler was trying to be the first-ever black owner of an NFL team. Not sure why, but craziness just followed me. Oh, I *so* needed to get this man out of my life!

Since I now knew that the line of credit I'd counted on wasn't real, I needed to create my own reserves for the company by selling off one of the sites. Then I could use those dollars and the cash reserves on our balance sheet to go to a bank- a *real* one this time- to get financed on all the stores. Once financed, I'd exercise the underlying purchase options on the properties and get Fowler done and *gone*.

The plan I came up with was to sell one of the sites I had in Mesa, Arizona; Fowler owned the underlying real estate on this site, but I had a purchase option to buy it from him directly for $3.3 million. I knew of a guy who wanted to buy the site for $4.8 million, so my thinking was to sell the one property, get the surplus of cash on hand, and get the financing I needed to buy Fowler out from the other sites.

I agreed to sell the site, and a month went by and my buyer for the Mesa site was ready to close. I did all the paperwork required with Fowler and the title company, got everything signed, and a day before the scheduled closing date the title company sent me a draft of the closing statement showing my company receiving approximately $1.5 million in funds when the site recorded the next day.

Even though I was losing a pretty good site, I was gaining the cash power needed to get Fowler out of my life. It was all set and ready to go the next day with the buyer. What could go wrong?

I've got to stop saying that.

Bright and early the next morning the title company called me.

"Mr. Gagliano," the lady on the phone said, "we are all set to record and close on the Mesa property, but I need you to bring in the shortfall of approximately seventy-five hundred dollars so we can record."

"You must be making a mistake," I said. "I'm the seller, not the buyer."

"I know who you are. I'm just following the instructions we received from Fowler's office this morning."

Overnight, Fowler had confirmed that my buyer had wired the $4.8 million in purchase money to the title company and that *all* my documents were completed as needed for a closing. That's when Fowler's plan went into action. Because of the March rent default that occurred a couple months earlier- that was *only* caused because Fowler didn't pay the requested draw on the line of credit, and I paid the rents on the seventh of the month- there was a clause in the leases on the properties that he "owned" that stated, "If a rent default ever occurs, the landlord maintains the right to request a $300,000 per site security deposit from the tenant."

With my buyer's $4.8 million now wired to the title company to buy the Mesa site, and all of the paperwork completed, Fowler's overall plan to conspire to take everything from me went in motion. Fowler had alerted the title company first thing in the morning that he was now demanding $1.5 million in security deposits be paid from the proceeds of this sale to cover security deposits on a two-day rent default that *he* caused in March.

I went from getting $1.5 million in badly needed company reserves to being told that morning that I *owed* $7500 just to close on the transaction. All this while knowing that I was still losing a great car washing site. Fowler outplayed me on this; he leveraged our phony friendship to gain information from me. And, I let him do it.

This was now war.

I'd heard the rumors that he was pond scum and a man of zero character, but I chose to overlook those rumors. Now it was all being very painfully verified. From that point forward, every time I spoke to him I recorded the phone calls. On most of the calls he was quite contrite, apologizing for what he did, blaming it on the stress of the Vikings deal coupled with the press and NFL putting pressure on him. I knew there were many articles berating his partnership with me because of the ASU sports bribery case, but Fowler's comments in public were always positive:

"What Mr. Gagliano did in the past is not what our partnership is about now. He is a good partner and a good tenant on some of my properties."

That's what he said publically. Privately he had an agenda. I needed him gone forever. So I called him up.

"What's it going to take to get you out of my life? What do I have to do?"

"Teach me how to operate and give me one of the sites," he replied.

I agreed. I chose a site we operated on 48th street and Chandler Blvd. in the Phoenix area; it was a pretty big store worth almost *five* million. Fowler already owned the underlying property for about $3.3 million, so to get him out of my life I was going to lose another site and in the process pay almost another *two* million.

Rewind for a second to ten months earlier, when all was going pretty well. Through another relationship I had, I was able to get the licensing rights to a crazy little product that I wanted to market hard for the Christmas season.

It was indeed another crazy entrepreneurial venture. But, that was me, a true deal junkie. It was a licensing agreement with porn star Jenna Jameson on a pubic hair trimmer. It was a nicely packaged novelty item that allowed you to trim your pubic hair areas into different shapes. I'd put $1.1 million into this venture, and Fowler $300,000. To market and create sales, I sponsored the Howard Stern radio show for Christmas season of 2003, and bought hundreds of radio and television spots. It was a neat little idea and I truly thought it would sell.

Man, was I ever *wrong*; it totally flopped. At the end of it I was just over $1.2 million in the hole on the deal with about 300,000 units of the product left in inventory. I had mispriced the product and neither Fowler nor I got our money back. What sales we had did nothing more than pay for the ad spots.

After I agreed to give Fowler the site on 48th and Chandler in exchange for my freedom from our partnership. I arranged to have my staff train his office people for a thirty-day period on how to run a car wash, C-Store, and gas station. For thirty days he had people at the site learning all aspects of the business, and while they were learning to operate, my attorneys and I worked towards completing the documents needed to end the business relationship between us.

Finally, the day came to turn possession of the site over to Fowler, but conveniently he wasn't around; he'd sent his *team* over to the site to count inventory, deal with me, and get the keys to the store. We counted inventory, took a reading of how much fuel was in the tanks, then his CFO wrote me a check for just over $200,000 for the items on site.

I signed all the transfer paperwork at the site, and we were ready to give Fowler's team the keys, but before we did I noticed that one of the documents that we had agreed to sign was not signed by Fowler. It was the document stating that the $300,000 he had invested in Jenna Jameson Hot trimmers was canceled and nothing was owed.

The locksmiths were at the site ready to change the locks, inventory was counted and paid for, but now I had to make a decision if I was going to give him the site or demand the $300,000 paid note signed prior. In my mind it was just a simple "Paid in Full" document for $300,000 he'd invested in a different project. He would already have the site, so what else could he possibly do to me?

I *really* must stop asking questions like that.

I decided to call up Fowler directly. He was in Colorado. I told him all was ready to go. Inventory done and paid for, but that I didn't have the paid in full note for the Hot Trimmers that we'd agreed to. Somehow his slick tongue managed to convince me that it was an oversight, and he would get it to me ASAP when he flew back to Arizona that night. Foolish me, I believed him and gave his people the keys to the store right then and there.

Sure enough, his words meant nothing. A couple of days later I was served with formal court papers claiming that I owed him the $300,000 investment; that he'd only invested the money into the Hot Trimmers Company because I had agreed to secure those dollars with my eighty percent ownership in the Shammy Man Car Washes operating company.

That formal court complaint was served to me in addition to another formal notice that same day, informing me that all of the remaining purchase options that I had in place with Fowler for me to buy the remaining real estate, were no longer valid due to the lease default that occurred in March of 2005.

This entire mess came from a two-day lease default in March 2005, solely caused because of *his* lack of funding the draw request I submitted on the line of credit.

He was a real piece of work.

I guess I wasn't as smart as I thought I was, so let this be a lesson to you when you decide whom to do business with, and how.

Yep, I'm viewed as the bad guy... I'm the "convicted felon"... Let me tell you that I would *much* rather have those labels than to have the same DNA running through my veins as runs through Fowler's, a guy who knowingly exploits people through lies and deceit just for personal gain. Just saying...

This episode doesn't excuse my poor past choices. But pushing the envelope to better a person's position versus outright deceit while hurting others in the process are *not* equal in my book. Of course, it should have been a very clear sign to me, looking back now at how lonely and empty this man was. Again, trust your gut...

We battled in the courts for a little while, and throughout that time I had security guards hired to patrol my sites at nighttime so he couldn't try to lock us out. I was able to maintain operation of the sites for another few months without paying him a dime, until finally he got me with a simple landlord-tenant claim that gave him immediate access to the sites. I knew I was going to lose at that hearing, but before that hearing, I had intentionally drained the sites of all the life left in them, taking out the POS systems, signage, some equipment, and most of the inventory, plus I gave away as many *free* car wash passes and annual passes as I could to our customer base.

If he wanted to operate *my* car washes, he'd have to replace all the systems, equipment, and honor a whole lot of free services. The year before I had those sites practically exploding with positive cash flow. By the time he got control of them, they were left with hardly a pulse.

Karma can really bite you in the rear when you aren't looking. It certainly had with me. The fake Super Bowl squares, the 900 numbers, the ASU point shaving—I'd like to think I learned from those past mistakes. I didn't want to be that guy any more, and when I got out of prison I tried to do things the right way. But Karma found me.

Its name was Fowler.

Karma plays fair, however. It found Fowler, too. He failed miserably in the car wash business and his other businesses started to fail as well. He was kicked to the curb in the Vikings deal only given a token spot as one of the many minority investors. In the years that followed others he'd cheated stood in line to drag him into court, and one group was successful in getting him deposed in late 2012.

In that deposition Fowler, who in 2005 claimed to the NFL on a financial statement to be worth in excess of $400 million, now had IRS tax liens on him, several bank foreclosures, and was on the verge of losing what sliver of ownership that he still had with the Vikings.

I guess every dog has his day, and in the end we are all going to be judged by only One; I somehow still find some peace knowing that Fowler will have that day.

As mad as I was in 2005, I always asked myself if I was "20 years to life mad." My answer was always, "Heck no!"

It's weird, but Fowler's desire to get my company taught me some very valuable life lessons, and proved to be, oddly enough, a fairly peaceful exit from the full service car wash business.

True, in total he cost me between fourteen and fifteen million dollars in real estate and business equity, but I had seen the writing on the wall for the car wash business. The entire industry was changing, and the consumers were moving to a more self-serve express model.

Fast forward a few years later to Fowler's operations in 2009, after the world's financial meltdown, when many full service car washes were lucky to survive. He'd placed loans on all of the sites he took from me and ended up losing tens of millions of dollars, and eventually losing the sites to the banks.

Remember this: beware the next time you plan to start up a business relationship with someone and that person smiles like you're old friends. Look very carefully where you step and try not to follow in my footsteps.

Chapter Fifteen:

Building Up Again - The World Falls Apart

Most of 2006 was spent in San Diego on the boat wallowing in guilt over my divorce. Oh, not because of a broken heart or lost love, but simply due to the breakup of the classic family unit. I never wanted my kids to have to say that their parents were divorced, but those last five years of my marriage I was just not happy. We lacked common ground.

The ASU scandal and conviction, prison, building a successful company only to lose it - all added up and took its toll. I needed to try to fix myself, rid myself of the broken family guilt that I was suffering from, and try to figure out how to use my talents to be the person in life I knew I was meant to be. That meant some alone time and a new start. I had to somehow break away from everything connected with my past life and figure out what path to pursue next.

Even with losing the company as I did, I still had a few bucks left, and some of the toys that I had acquired along the way. So, I tried to relax in San Diego, and that summer bought a bigger brand new boat, and spent the bulk of my time watching the race horses I owned run at Del Mar and Santa Anita. I wanted to focus on my talents. My strength was in creating concepts. And, being a "visionary" to build a company. So I came up with a plan to get ahead of the curve in the car wash business and to open a chain of express car washes. I still owned a property in Chandler, Arizona that was perfect for an express car wash, so that year in San Diego I created the concept of the Fast Lane Auto Spa. It was a quality express car wash with *free* vacuum for the customers to use.

Construction on my first Fast Lane Auto Spa began in late 2006. This was also the time that my cousin and old Shammy Man director of operations, Joe Scarzone, asked if he could buy the last full-service car wash site I owned. It was one of the properties that I'd acquired in 2001 in Mesa, Arizona that I'd managed to keep clear of Fowler's paws. It never did all that well, just simply stayed afloat, but it was a nice piece of real estate, worth about $3.0 million. I agreed to sell it to Scarzone for $2.5 million.

Scarzone got a loan to buy the site from Alliance Bank in Arizona for about two million dollars and approached me to 'carry back" $500,000 so he could pay me those funds later. I agreed, and in late 2006 he purchased the site from me. Since I did really want to do things right, when it closed I listed the full purchase price of $2.5 million on my personal income tax returns.

Construction was completed for the first Fast Lane Auto Spa in 2007. I completely overbuilt the site, which included fifteen hundred square feet of second floor office space with personal showers and bathrooms. I even had private parking for myself and the staff. Total build out for this project was just under five million bucks.

By the time the first Fast Lane Auto Spa opened, I entered into a joint venture agreement with a company called Glimcher Ventures Southwest, owned by David Glimcher, former CEO of the Glimcher REIT, a publically traded real estate company. Our agreement planned to scale the concept, and set out a development plan to grow to thirty sites in a thirty-six month period. We hired a full team of designers, architects, contractors, and attorneys to make it happen.

My past experiences with Fowler had made me a *lot* wiser in how I wanted a deal like this to be structured. Glimcher provided the debt financing but we *both* owned the real estate; Glimcher owned eighty percent and I owned the remaining twenty, which meant I had to put in twenty percent of the equity for the sites as well. However, I would own one hundred percent of all of the operations.

Now all was set to once again build, own, and operate a large, successful company. I figured I was a lot smarter this time and wouldn't be making the same mistakes twice. I knew where the car wash industry was going, so I endeavored to stay ahead of the curve.

With my Fast Lane joint venture with Glimcher now in full motion, together we were able to open two other sites, with another one a month away from construction completion. Two others were just beginning construction, while the land for another two were just closing escrow. With the joint venture in place, a total of ten sites were either opened, under construction, or about to start. It was all working out pretty well. We were well on our way to completing the thirty sites in thirty-six months.

Then the fourth quarter of 2008 happened and the financial world fell apart. It was like doom itself had come calling.

As wealthy as I thought David Glimcher and his partner John Scottenstein were, they were just two guys who were *highly* leveraged at the wrong time. The majority of Glimcher's wealth was held in the Glimcher REIT - NYSE shares (GRT), which in the fourth quarter of 2008 went from about $20 per share down to a dime.

This was not a good time for the financial world to implode on these two. They had several large shopping centers under construction, and all of the loans- including the Fast Lane ones- were collateralized by their financial statements. When the stock value fell through the basement, every bank Glimcher dealt with called their notes due and started foreclosing.

It was a blood bath, one I had a twenty percent stake in. Without warning, and to no fault of anyone in that partnership, I was about to lose the equity I'd placed in the sites, and the entire partnership as well.

Lehman Brothers and two of the Big Three car companies filed for bankruptcy. The Dow dropped down to 7000- about *half* what it had been. Glimcher, of course, filed for bankruptcy protection, and in the middle of all this mess our partnership lost the sites to the banks. All the effort I'd put into those sites for the past two years, and about three million dollars in equity, all gone...

It was a *really* bad time.

The Glimcher business partnership was now dead. After the pure hell I experienced with Fowler, and now the world financial market collapse, all I had left to my name was the Chandler Fast Lane site that I'd built for $5.0 million, with a $3.6 million loan on it. The problem was that the loan was a construction *only* loan, and the construction lender was already past the maturity date and demanding to be paid off immediately.

Somehow, in the middle of this financial crisis, I had to find $3.6 million to pay off the construction lender at a time when the banks were not even thinking about lending money. They were all just in survival mode... as was I.

Chapter Sixteen:

Investigated - Again

With the financial world in complete chaos, no money, no bank to turn to for help, and a mound of debt, what was I to do? Only one option was open to me and that was another SBA government loan. I'd done two already in the past, both with my dad as the principal, but after successfully beating colon cancer in 2005, now my dad was battling liver cancer.

I called him up to discuss what was needed and he replied with just one question.

"I don't have to put up any money, do I?"

"No, Dad. I only need you to be the principal on the SBA loan, just like before."

With the DOW down to 7000 and the economy in the toilet, even my dad was feeling the pinch. But with my assurance in place of no money needed, he replied as I'd hoped he would.

"Joey, you're the trustee of the estate, do what's needed and let me know when you need me."

With that done, I had the attorneys form the entities needed, then called the SBA department at Wells Fargo Bank, and the SBA offices in Phoenix, arranging a meeting with *both* of them in person. I wanted to explain the situation clearly so there would be no mistakes.

"My father is suffering from liver cancer. Now, he is the borrower but because of my history operating car washes, I'll be managing the site. Also, while my father is being treated for his cancer, I will act as the point of contact. Is this understood?"

Nods were given, assurances rendered, and all agreed. I paid them an application fee to start, and the bank began the underwriting for the loan. During this process, my dad actually had to get fingerprinted for the loan and spoke with four different bankers from Wells Fargo who had called him directly in Vegas to confirm a few lender questions and verify some of his assets. Even the SBA office in Phoenix spoke with him directly about details and items needed.

A short time after the underwriting, and after the bank had completed three separate appraisals for the property, Wells Fargo and the SBA approved the loan for approximately $3.5 million.

The loan documents were delivered to the title company on the same day that my dad was scheduled for a chemo treatment in Las Vegas. So, beat down with chemo, my dad just told me to handle it.

My cousin Joe Scarzone's ex-wife was the branch manager of the title company the bank was using, so on a Friday morning, rather than title formally demanding that all bank loan documents be signed in their presence, Scarzone got some special treatment and arranged via his ex-wife for title to release and hand over to him directly all of the bank loan documents with instructions to have them delivered back to the title office by Monday morning, signed.

Sounds straightforward enough but here is where I made another bad choice in life. I *do* seem to have a lot of them. But then if I didn't, you wouldn't have this book to read.

Since I didn't have an official bank power of attorney in place with my dad, the *best* thing I should have done with those loan documents would have been to go to Las Vegas and sit with my dad while he signed them himself. But my dad was weak from the chemo treatments and I didn't feel like making the trip. Besides, I knew that I had my dad's blessing to sign the documents as needed, just like we've done many times before on many other loans.

So over the weekend, I made, what I then thought to be, a seemingly innocent decision. The consequences of that life choice would later prove nearly fatal my family and me.

I arranged for the documents to be signed on my father's (and mother's) behalf. And, allowed for Scarzone to complete their signatures.

I signed because I was a manager of the operating entity that was approved and underwritten on the loan. And, because I was also personally guarantying the loan. Scarzone then signed his personal name as an operating manager as well. With my approval, he also signed my mom and dad's name directly on all the loan documents where needed.

He did the signing for my parents instead of me because I have a left-handed slant to my writing and I thought it was best that the documents had a different style for their signatures. I remember him practicing the styles many times before signing the actual documents, each time asking for my approval.

Legally I could have signed the names even with my left handed slant. Typically, however, when signing for someone else, you get a power of attorney. I didn't have it. I also didn't need it. But, I didn't want my weird signature to gum up the works and raise unwanted questions.

I basically leveraged the personal relationship Scarzone had with the title company to get them to look the other way on specific required protocol. Pushing to get them to release the documents from their possession. And, pushing for what I wanted so this loan could fund. I knew I should have gotten the power of attorney, if I did, none of this would have ever been questioned.

I was living in the grey area. Again...

After the documents were signed, I took things even further, and I found a notary to notarize the two different "Joseph Gagliano" signatures on the loan documents; the ones for me and the ones for my dad.

Heck, on that Saturday afternoon, I even got this girl to notarize my mom's signature as well because I asked her to. That girl probably had no idea she was breaking the law and I didn't exactly bother to bring it up to her. All she knew was what I told her, and in her mind saw was the name Joseph Gagliano on my ID showed. She just never even realized that there were actually two different Joseph Gagliano's.

The title company received the signed documents on Monday morning as requested and the loan funded the next day. Immediately after that I paid off the construction lender. 100% of the funds went to pay off the construction lender. No funds were taken out of the loan or went to me. In spite of losing just about everything to Fowler and having the rest taken away in the Glimcher venture, I thought I had survived, and was almost relieved at that point to have *anything* left for my family during this world financial mess.

Then in 2009 the economy got even worse. Consumers were starting to have real concerns about spending *anything*, including five bucks for a car wash, which meant that the Chandler site I'd fought so hard to keep in place was starting to feel the pressures as well.

I was paying 8.25% on the SBA loan to Wells Fargo Bank, so I called up the banker who did my loan- a guy by the name of Will Frazier- and told him that I needed the interest rate modified or I was going to move the loan. I was bluffing, of course, because I had no other options. But, I had a decent relationship with the man, so he quite candidly gave me an answer.

"I'll get you the interest reduction. It will take two months, but it'll get done. Just *please* don't move the loan because if you do, and the loan is *not* in place at the Wells Fargo bank for twelve months, then I'd have to pay back my commission from the deal."

I really felt bad for the guy. He'd fought hard to get me my loan placed, so I decided to leave him alone for the two months and let him get me the rate reduction. He told me that the new rate would be 5.25%, which translated into about an $8000 monthly reduction.

Two months went by and still no word from Will. I called him and he assured me it would be done inside of next month, so when the next month came and I still had no rate reduction, I decided to stop making payments to the bank. I felt like I was being lied to and that Will was obviously trying to push me aside just to get to the 12-month mark so he could keep his fees.

The next month the payment was overdue and I got a call from Will's boss, Angela Bowman.

"Mr. Gagliano, we are concerned as to why haven't you made your payment," she asked.

"I'm waiting on a three-point reduction in the interest rate that your employee, Mr. Frazier, had promised me both verbally and in writing."

"*Mr.* Gagliano," she said in a stern voice, "at this point you have *three* options. First, to pay the current note, second to pay the loan off, or third to hand me the keys."

Sales were *really* suffering at this point, so I stood my ground.

"Well, Miss Bowman, if those are my only options, I guess I will see you in court for promissory reliance and lender liability claims, then."

She didn't seem to like that much; I could practically hear her indignant huff over the phone before she hung up.

With the economy limiting sales at the site, and real estate prices plummeting, my plan was to let Wells Fargo file whatever they wanted in the courts and keep delaying the hearings with motions, all while keeping the doors open at the site to keep bringing in revenue. I wanted to either force them into a settlement or give myself enough time to create some options.

But they wouldn't settle. Why *would* they? The banks were just given *TARP* bailout money by the federal government. Sure, the government said the dollars they gave out through the TARP bailout plan had to be paid back, but it was government money for the banks to use as needed.

You might have thought this would make the banks more likely to deal with existing borrowers, but it didn't. It just gave them a bigger cushion. Wells was in first position on the loan, with about $1.5 million at risk. The SBA guaranteed the rest. Wells decided to play hardball.

The government bailed out the banks, and in the process allowed the banks to dig their heels in further with borrowers that were in trouble.

I knew that with the loan I had placed, I took the banks money, and in doing so, that those dollars needed to be repaid. But, I also knew that because of the worldwide financial crisis we were in, that I was a borrower in real trouble. One that could have used the help that the TARP plan was intended for. But, things just didn't work out that way.

Our Government seems to have a "special" way of giving a person an umbrella when it's sunny out only to take it away when it rains.

So I created my own plan. David Beckham, who had become a trusted friend, had a fairly good relationship with a Wells Fargo executive and was told that if Wells Fargo got the site back from me, that they would then schedule a sale within thirty days afterwards. With that news, my attorney and I decided to allow Wells Fargo to take possession of the site. David and I planned to attend the auction so that I could possibly buy back the site. I had investors who were going to buy and own the real estate side, and I would operate it. This time I was playing the bank's games, and felt that if they wanted to back pedal on spoken words, then I should attempt to own it at a discounted price.

After all, no one knew the site better than me.

With the economy the way it was, it would certainly sell for far less than the $3.5 million I owed to Wells Fargo, which would leave me in a better possession. With that plan in place, I allowed Wells Fargo to get me into a courtroom, and after milking the site's revenue for another few months, I conceded possession of the site back to them.

Once Wells Fargo got the site back, the auction was scheduled for four weeks later. David was in weekly communication with the department at Wells Fargo that was handling the transaction. All was in place but then the Wednesday before the Friday auction David received a call.

The auction was canceled.

Without public notice, the bank had decided to sell the site directly to one of their private clients for $1.5 million, which was not even close to the value of the property. They never even *tried* to get the best price that they could, and never tried to recoup any dollars for the SBA. They only wanted to make one of their private clients happy because, in the end, as long as they got theirs, any other money lost didn't matter to them. They sold it far below value, got their money, and left the SBA and the government portion high and dry.

The SBA ended up losing $2.1 million on the loan because of the dirty hands at Wells Fargo. Had they auctioned the property in a public forum to get the best end result, the losses would have been far less. Meanwhile, the TARP bailouts did *nothing* to help the people in trouble. It only provided more profit for the banks to reset their balance sheets and pay bigger bonuses to executives.

That was my last asset; now all was gone. I didn't know what to think. Maybe I was cursed. I thought maybe I was indeed just a bad person being punished for my bad choices in life. The ASU scandal, building a successful company but being a poor steward of those blessings, losing the company to Fowler because of wanting to prove others wrong about me, the lost years and money from the badly-timed Glimcher joint venture, ending an unhappy marriage while thinking I was hurting my kids, and now losing the last asset I had - it was enough to get to anybody.

I was a wreck, and certainly not thinking clearly anymore, either in business or my personal life. I'd had it.

Chapter Seventeen:

The $90 Dinner Bill at Chili's

In December of 2009 I threw in the towel and filed for personal bankruptcy. I listed any and all debts I'd signed over the years, including the manager's signature and personal guarantees I'd signed on the Wells Fargo and SBA Chandler car wash property loan. I was done with that business. With the economy the way it was, I knew it was time to reinvent myself in some other way and make a fresh start.

I was out of the car wash business for the first time in *thirteen* years, and looking for something new. So, I took a stab at E-commerce by building an advertising based website. Knowing little about this space, I put together a plan and budgeted the concept to be complete at about $300,000.

Man, was I ever wrong! So wrong, in fact, that I had to bring in a couple of business partners for additional funds, including my sister. Fifteen months later, we were well over $1.4 million spent and facing the realization that without more large amounts of capital there was just *no way* we were ever going to penetrate that market space. Of course with my passion for pushing a square peg into a round hole I probably would have kept pushing the concept forward making it work, except for one major thing.

Just when I believed I had hit rock bottom, and learned to adapt to my new world with the toys and cash all gone, for a brief moment, I felt relief. Relief that it couldn't get any worse. Struggling to get by was new to me now. But I always had confidence in myself. That confidence quickly evaporated when, my dad called me up in late 2010.

"Joey, two FBI agents just visited me and your mother."

Five days prior to this FBI visit, my parents had driven down to Arizona for the weekend to watch my daughter perform in one of her many theater plays. After the play we all went out to have dinner at Chili's. Chili's was my then 14-year-old daughter's favorite place.

When the bill came, I grabbed it from the waiter but my mom wanted to pay it. When the bill comes to a table, it's an engrained habit for me to reach for it, broke or not. I was trying to be thoughtful and not have my parents pay for things, so I got a bit more forceful and I guess even raised my voice some when I said, "I got it."

Now, my dad is my hero; he and I have just always clicked. But the relationship between my mom and me, while most times loving on the exterior, was always strained, mainly because I don't buy into her usual soapbox drama. So there I was, raising my voice a bit over a lousy $90 dinner bill at Chili's in front of my kids. Not my best moment, but my stress ruled in those days.

After dinner we made plans to meet at church in the morning and get together for a brunch before my parents started their drive back to Vegas. But the next morning my dad called to tell me that they'd woken up early and driven back to Vegas because my mom was mad that I'd yelled at her in front of the kids. My parents left town without saying goodbye to me or the kids simply because my mom was mad about this nonsense.

That started the stalemate between my parents and me. This was not the first time it'd happened. However, it usually was because my mom and I disagreed over something stupid and my dad would then be forced to side with her just to keep sanity in his home. Our standoff over who was going to break first and call the other had begun.

This family stalemate was still going on when the FBI agents came calling to my parents' home. Stalemate or not, even now I have no idea why my parents would have invited them in, especially after the lessons painfully learned from the ASU case. But they did... FYI for all the kids at home reading this, know that *nothing* good can ever come from FBI agents asking questions no matter *how polite* they pretend to be. They are always on a mission.

Timing in life is everything. And personally, I can't help but think the agents were invited in to talk simply because at that time, my mom was angry with me. Mom always loves making a point and in the process making sure that everyone around her knows what it is. I focus on not believing that my own mother would knowingly put me in that position, but it's hard not to. I've read the FBI statements and the interviews so many times I could recite them. The agents were in the house and asked my parents questions about the SBA loan we did on the Chandler property in 2008. Then, showed them the loan documents with their own signatures signed by Scarzone.

In 2008, when that Chandler SBA loan was completed, it was arguably the *worst* year of my parents' life. Dad had undergone three surgeries; two for liver cancer and one for a herniated disk in his neck. He also had twelve separate chemotherapy treatments to shrink the cancer in between the surgeries. With all that going on, the SBA loan and its details had little to no importance to my parents. They had gone through a medical nightmare. Now, with FBI agents in their home four years later, my dad was 74 and my mom 67. Neither one was very likely to remember that loan deal when put on the spot.

FBI agents always come to your door for a reason.

These agents eased their way into my aging parents' house by giving them the impression of simply being there to help. When they showed my parents the SBA loan documents and asked, "Is this your signature on these loan documents," my parents would not lie. And there was no reason for them to do so.

"No it's not," my dad replied, then in the next breath added, "but I do have a lot of business dealings with my son in Arizona."

There's a reason why FBI agents don't use recording devices for a conversation. When it's not recorded they get to write down their own version of the story and comments, selectively omitting and tilting the conversation to best suit their needs. After a ten or twenty-minute interview, what the agents wrote down in their 302 interview document was that, "Mr. and Mr. Gagliano stated that was not their signature on the $3.5 million dollar loan documents. And they have not talked to their son in quite some time because of a family argument."

I'm sure that FBI 302 interview painted a picture to the U.S Attorney of a dysfunctional family that didn't communicate or work together.

Why were the FBI agents at my parents' house in the first place? Because of my name and its history in that office. They apparently felt compelled to investigate my bankruptcy filing of December 2009. They were looking for fraud. When I filed, as the attorneys had advised me, I listed *all* of my debts on the petition as well as any items I had signed for, including the personal guarantees on the Wells Fargo / SBA loan. Apparently the FBI agents found it a challenge to understand that I was, in fact, on the personal guarantees for the loan underwritten by Wells Fargo. And, because of that I did have the proper rights to list the SBA loan on the bankruptcy filings, and thus ask for the relief of debt.

However, because of the past ASU felony, and my name held to a higher standard in the FBI office, I was an easy target for them. Once they had figured out that I did indeed list the bankruptcy petition correctly, they couldn't leave well enough alone and sought to find other ways to make a point.

They went about it by looking into the two-million dollar loan my cousin Joe Scarzone took out to buy my last full-service car wash in Mesa, Arizona off of me. Now, I never did anything on securing that loan. I never talked to the bank he used. Nor did I care how or why he got the loan. All I did was agree to sell him the site for $2.5 million, then my cousin went out and got the two million dollar loan and I carried back $500,000. Heck, I even reported the full amount of $2.5 million sale on my personal tax returns.

Apparently after Scarzone got the loan he only made a few payments here and there, then defaulted. That default, coupled with me listing that asset on my bankruptcy petition, got the FBI over to interview him for suspicion of bank fraud. According to the FBI report of that interview, their conversation quickly went from getting answers and details about the loan *he* obtained and defaulted on to what he could tell them about the seller, *me...*

During their interview with Scarzone, they selectively chose to forget the fraudulent ways he may have obtained his bank loan that he defaulted on and asked him one fatal question.

"What can you tell us about Mr. Gagliano?"

After all the years Scarzone and I worked together and everything we did together, the *only* thing my cousin could come up with was to make some stuff up about me using my Dad as a shill to obtain the Chandler SBA loan in 2008 without my dad's knowledge.

When I read the report, I couldn't believe it. The same loan he was claiming to the FBI that I fraudulently obtained, was the *same* loan that he personally guaranteed, and had signed both of my parents' names directly on. Seriously!!!

Now, with his back was against the wall for bank fraud, he wanted to spin it to look like I'd used my dad as a shill without his knowledge (which wasn't true) because I wasn't able to get a loan due to my felony record (also not true). Funny how that worked; perception sadly becomes reality.

FBI agents are motivated to bring cases forward. If they manage to bring a case against a prior felon, it's even better. When they do, they get *two* gold stars on their foreheads instead of just the one.

That thought process quickly made chasing after Scarzone's fraudulent two-million dollar loan quickly lose its luster when presented with the opportunity to get a past felon from a high profile case. It is always easier to convict someone with a prior conviction and it makes for better press, too.

The FBI went on to investigate, interviewing people to back up some details. They interviewed our business attorneys, who clearly stated to them that they set up the entities used with my dad as the manager at my dad's direct request.

They talked to all of the bankers at Wells Fargo whom we'd dealt with for the loan, and four out of six bankers stated in their FBI interviews that they spoke with my father directly during the underwriting process.

The government knew that my dad was personally fingerprinted for the SBA loan and that I'd completed nine other loans with my father over the years on various car washes and homes. They also knew that my parents received several benefits from the businesses I'd owned over the years from being on payroll, vacations, cars, insurance, bonuses, and so on.

But instead of looking at all that, they focused instead on Scarzone's lies, and they were very selective about what they wrote and took from my parents' words. They used lines like, "They didn't recognize their signatures on the loan documents." It was this highly selective/guarded type of "evidence" that the FBI then brought to the office of the U.S. Attorney in Phoenix to bring an indictment against me.

Looking back, I invited this trouble. I allowed the grey areas to be in the forefront of my dealings. Now, when something like this arises, know that every "I" is dotted and all "T's" are crossed. I learned this painful lesson for the second time. This time the hard way.

Chapter Eighteen:

Attorneys Are Born Liars

When I discovered that I was once again the target of a federal investigation, this time around unlike the ASU case, I knew first and foremost that there was no fraud, no intent to deceive, or anything improper done except for allowing the signing of my parents' names by Scarzone- which I had their approval to do. In fact, looking at the overall deal, I had lost over a million dollars on that project that they now claimed was fraudulent.

My fault was failing to then realize the legalities of my laziness. We all should be cognoscente of this trait. I knew for years that the prior felony had placed a larger target on my back. As time passed, I became less aware.

Fraud usually equates to some sort of profits. Not in this case, hell, I was broke. Lousy timing, too, because fighting for my innocence was not going to be an easy thing to do with no money.

What was my only hope? In my opinion: the facts. Unlike the ASU case where I knew I was actually guilty of a crime, this time I felt certain that the facts that would clearly show any U.S. attorney that I did nothing wrong. And once any U.S. attorney had all the facts, there was no way on God's green earth that any sane person could bring a criminal case against me. I was the trustee on these deals and authorized to make decisions. I just needed someone to help the government understand that my family acted as one large "bucket," helping each other out whenever needed. That we operated as a team. Together.

The concept of a family unit and family helping family was going to be a difficult concept for the government to grasp. Their perceptions in this case were their realities. The statements made by Scarzone, along with the untimely visit to my parents' home - that set their stage.

It was late 2010. Who did I go to for legal help in this mess? The *same* attorney that I'd used for the ASU case. Tom Connelly. Okay, not the perfect choice, but remember, I had no money. Sometimes the devil you think you know always seems better than the unknown. Besides, because he knew me and understood some things I did business wise, I was confident that he would work with me on the fees needed.

So, I worked out a flat fee deal for $50,000 where he'd let me pay it out in five $10,000 installments. I literally did *all* the work for him, and gave him all the ammo he would need to present to the U.S attorney's office. Ammo which at the least would have raised serious concerns about their case.

I became stressed out with just the *thought* of having to fight a case again or the possibilities of going back to prison. I would work all day and night searching for files, pulling data from old hard drives, and searching my prior staff's computers. I paid computer techs to retrieve old emails and any records I might need, all to show to the government that their notions of fraud were unfounded.

I found emails between my dad and me concerning the loan, and emails to the attorney that I'd copied my dad on; in these we discussed the structure of the entities, the closing, and the loan documents. I found emails from my dad the day before the closing asking me if there was anything he could do, as well as an email from him the day after closing asking how everything had gone.

In addition to all the emails, I also pulled files showing the nine previous loans my father and I had done together so that the government would see that this Chandler loan was not a "one off" occurrence. I needed them to see that there was a long history of our family helping one another and doing business together. I then gave *all* of this information to Connelly, who simply needed to present these facts to the U.S. attorney. A monkey with a crank music box could have done that, especially a monkey being paid a $50,000 fee.

I know you're asking, why do I keep trusting these people? Well, in this case, I had no other options. Money talks in the legal world and I had none at that time.

Connelly told me many times during the almost sixteen months he "represented me" that he had a *strong* personal relationship with the U.S. attorney who was handling my case and that he would be able to "make this issue go away" for me because of that relationship.

Then in the *same* breath he'd tell me that he needed more money; because apparently such relationships don't come cheap, and that this "favor" he would be calling in for me should be costing me a ton more.

At that point I honestly didn't care how the FBI investigation went away. If it ended due to the facts I gave Connelly - fine. If it ended by way of personal favors and relationships—that was fine, too. I just wanted to be out of the crosshairs.

All while I was being told about his strong relationship inside the U.S attorney's offices, he *never* presented any of the information or facts outlining all the events to them.

With one prior already in my history, I knew that *if* I got indicted again and was forced to fight for my innocence, that it would be ugly. I was scared to death at the possibility of returning to federal prison, so I did anything Connelly asked me to do.

Connelly liked the E-commerce company I was developing so I gave him a 5% equity stake in it. He needed more money, and, since I didn't personally have any, I created loan documents with my company to pay him back large amounts of interest for small-change loans he made to my company for 30 to 60 day periods

Connelly needed access to a building in Tucson where he said an old client of his left money in the ceiling before he was sent to prison, so I spent four weeks in Tucson gaining access to that building under a false pretense to do that for him as well.

When he needed institutional financing introductions for a few real estate deals he was trying to put together, I introduced him to several groups that I had relationships with.

Anything he leaned on me for, I pushed to get done. I viewed this guy as the one who was going to help me avoid a whole bunch of headaches. So, my goal was to not say NO to him when he asked for something.

And all while, he hardly ever spoke to me about the ongoing investigation against me. When the topic *did* come up, he'd reply with something like, "Don't worry about it; I have it handled. The U.S. attorney is doing me a personal favor on this to help, Joe." He said that many times in front of me, my then-girlfriend, and a few of my friends as well.

He even boldly stated to me and others that the Arizona U.S. Attorney and his wife often went to dinner together with him and his wife, and that the man was thinking of leaving the governments office to partner up with him in the private sector. Being from Chicago, and knowing how the political wheel is greased by personal relationships, I bought into this and assumed that the "favor" was being called in and this nonsense would go away.

December 27, 2011 is a date I remember well, because not only was it my dad's birthday, it was also the day Connelly called saying that he wanted to meet me in his office. Once I got there, he told me that the U.S. attorney called him and said that he was planning to indict me after the first of the year.

"Are you *kidding me?!*" I screamed "How could anyone indict me after seeing the evidence, files, and documents I gave you to show him?"

"Joe, I never showed them those things. I didn't want to show them our cards." He said.

"*What* cards? I didn't do anything wrong here. I'm not trying to take the government to trial and put myself through business and personal *suicide!*"

But even as I said those words out loud, it became painfully clear what his plan was, for without missing a beat, he said to me,

"Joe, I will need five hundred thousand to get all ready for the trial. This trial will be the swan song of my career, because after I beat the government for you I plan to retire as an attorney."

That last part took real balls to say in my presence.

Swan song? Really?

I knew then I was in trouble, and that this guy had only been milking me for whatever he could get, with absolutely no regard for me, my family, or what happened next.

This was the same guy who would give me a big hug and kiss on the cheek whenever he saw me, asked about my kids, and told me he loved me like a brother. You have to be a real piece of self-serving pond scum to do things like that while keeping someone trapped beneath a veil of fear.

I put all my desperate faith into him for the close to sixteen months he "represented" me. I'd already paid him well with money I struggled to get. I did every crazy favor asked of me along the way. Now, I was broke. And, was now being told that I was going to be indicted again. I desperately needed to do something ASAP, but with everyone still in holiday mode, the only idea I came up with was to fight this battle myself, to personally prepare affidavits from people who knew the facts. And to hand deliver them to the FBI and U.S. Attorney's office to show my innocence.

I was able to get nine affidavits from different people together that clearly stated the facts, history of the loans, and details on the Chandler loan. With these delivered directly to the U.S. attorney's offices by me, it was clear in my mind that this U.S. attorney would now know what happened was *not* as he perceived the facts to be via the Scarzone statements.

During the New Year's holiday, I managed to get affidavits done by three different attorneys involved in the deal, one from my dad, one from my sister, and the rest from people who knew about the deal as well.

Yeah, it was a last ditch effort, my Hail Mary to avoid an indictment. I knew that delivering documents from me directly to the government was a risk. But I was out of time and out of options.

Chapter Nineteen:

The Pain Within

A few months earlier, my then-girlfriend became my fiancé. Even with all this trash and chaos going on in my life, through some extreme ups and downs, she still stuck by my side. With her saying "yes" even with all the insurmountable stress of a possible indictment, I tried to remain the optimist, thinking all would work itself out as needed. With that, I sold a few equity points in the e-commerce company to put a few dollars together so that in early January of 2012 we could move in together to a beautiful home in North Scottsdale via a deal I struck on a lease purchase.

On the surface things seemed great, but I knew that what I was facing was shaping up to be a complete mess. I was like a ticking time bomb awaiting the New Year's ball to drop in Times Square. I couldn't enjoy my life, my kids, my home, or the time I had together with my fiancé. I couldn't even focus on earning a living. The only thing I managed to do successfully was live in a daily state of fear with thoughts of going through the federal criminal and prison system again. I kept seeing the headlines in my mind while knowing the pain there'd be in my wife-to-be's eyes, and the eyes of my kids when I'd have to tell them the details.

I could only focus on the indictment, the potential of a pending trial, and the possibility of going back to prison.

Sure enough, my fears became a reality. On February 20th, 2012, I was indeed formally indicted in Arizona on seven counts of committing bank fraud, wire fraud, and false loan and credit applications. The charges were patently ludicrous; for instance, they accused me of overstating my father's assets on the application, which I did not—nor did I need to. They claimed my father wasn't aware of the loan, and on and on.

I was absolutely *sick,* depressed, walking around in a daze, and focused on how to fix things. I was absent with my kids, avoided the few friends who stood by me, and abandoned the E-commerce company into which I and my partners had invested a ton of money.

Worst of all, I was rotten at home as well. So much so that, after many arguments and me basically daring my fiancé to move out, she actually did. On the first of June in 2012, I was all alone, under indictment, flat broke, with no legal representation, and looking at *years* of prison time for something I know I didn't do.

In my mind, it was 1997 all over again. The newspapers picked up my indictment and ran with it. People I thought I had personal relationships with never returned my calls, business relationships I'd worked hard to forge via overcoming my prior felony label went missing-in-action. The information age is inescapable; there's nowhere to hide no matter how hard you want to. This indictment was business suicide. I was a pariah.

Looking back, it was eye opening to see how many people I held close avoided me. They either felt guilt by association or shame for the association. It became an easier out for them to believe what they were reading about me then to pick up the phone and call me. When I was rich and successful, the phone rang and calls were promptly returned. When the tide took its turn, most people in my life became eerily quiet. Another life lesson learned, this one about loyalty and self-serving interest.

Now this time around, though, my parents were older and unable to fight the good fight by my side. My sister was already knee-deep with me from investing in the E-commerce site and helping me to pay Connelly a part of the $50,000, and my brother and I didn't speak due to our difference in family and world views. My ex-wife and I decided not to tell the kids anything because I didn't want to stress them out over things that had an uncertain outcome.

For the first time in 43 years, I was alone.

Very alone.

I had no options on where or who to turn to. I was filled with bitterness towards my cousin Joe Scarzone for turning on me. After nearly ten years of us working together, side by side, giving him equity in the companies, vacations together, and sharing many personal experiences, he makes up a story to personally hurt my family and me because his back was against the wall. A bitter pill to swallow indeed.

My dad took these charges very hard. I know he felt that he should never have given those FBI agents the time of day, and he was greatly saddened that his own words were twisted and used to hurt me. My mom, though, seemed indifferent to everything. Her actions spoke louder than what she ever said to my face. I lean towards believing that when I lost my company, hit the hard times, and stopped being able to provide financially for the entire family, I basically lost my status as the Golden Child. They'd come to expect that largesse from me, and when I could no longer provide it, they all felt a bit cheated.

For many years, I was the one my family would turn to for help, advice, and to get things done they needed or dreamt about. They would often just call my assistant Kerri for things directly and speak to her more than they would to me. I never said no; if I could do something I always did. Even if I didn't have something they needed, I would most times aggressively go find it.

Back in 2004, when things were going somewhat well for me, my sister and her family were struggling. They had four boys trying to make it on a very limited income. She called me up one day. Told me that she always wanted to own a day care center. So, I told her to find a location.

A week later, she called back and said she had one selected. On a moment's notice, I'd emptied my bank account because my sister needed the seed money to buy her first building and start a company.

Once she opened the doors, I made developing her company my second daily job for years in addition to providing her with internal professional resources as well. That company turned out well; it now has multiple locations. And she paid me back the dollars I gave her through an SBA loan that I later structured for her to obtain.

But when the indictment was issued against me, I called my sister, told her about the situation, and my need for help. She flat out turned me down. Saying that her and her husband didn't want to go any further with me because they still had dollars out in the e-commerce company.

Isn't that funny?

I always gave and gave. Usually without any expectation of return. With my sister I gave while knowing that if her business had failed, I would most likely have never seen a penny of my money back. And, I knew I could live with that.

That thinking went along with my learned warped sense of money. I always thought that if I had it, everyone I loved in my circle would never go without. I wrongly assumed they felt the same way. When things went bad for me, I expected strangers to turn their backs on me. That I could live with. I just never thought my family would turn away.

My sister's business worked out for her. I will always be proud of what she fought to build. But, I will always remember that when my freedom was in jeopardy, when I was the one who needed help from a vicious attack, I stood alone.

She wasn't the only one who stood back. *No one* from my family was there. That is perhaps the most painful part of my struggles, and one I still deal with today. Memories seem to be very selective; people

you love can manage to forget all the good things you've done for them over the years, then dwell on the few speed bumps hit along the way.

I was a boat afloat in a sea of depression. With all that I lost, the biggest loss I focused on was that of my fiancé, Tracy. That left a pit the size of the Grand Canyon in my stomach. Even with all the fear and trials I knew lay ahead, I felt if there was *any* way I was ever going to live again and be the person I've always known I could be, I felt I had to have Tracy by my side.

But that was one *BIG* challenge. She has a very strong personality, and I had hurt her and let her down in many ways over the years. I prayed all this pain would simply end and I could press restart. I prayed that if there was *ever* a way that she could give me just one more chance that she would…

Or perhaps if it was just not meant for me to get some peace.

Chapter Twenty:

The Pit of Darkness

After the indictment but before arraignment, I ditched Connelly and hired a new law firm, Petti and Briones. I met with Fred Petti and Patti Briones at their offices in early March. Fred was in his early fifties, an ex U.S. attorney who'd gone into private practice. He was from an Italian family in Ohio, he completely understood the dynamics of an Italian family and the "what's mine is ours" mentality my family had shared. We clicked; there was a lot of common ground. So, despite my financial situation, Fred and Patti agreed to represent me.

There is a reason why people in the criminal world with money are not treated or sentenced in the same ways as the have-nots. It's due to the strength and power of the attorneys they are able to retain. At this point I was completely *broke*, but I think that Fred and Patti picked up on my history, that I had made a few bucks in my life and that if I got my head clear, I probably had the ability to do so again. So, because they were simply good people and knew where I was coming from, they agreed to go to war with me against the U.S attorney's office.

Most of 2012 was spent reviewing and gathering more facts, after which Fred and Patti would shove those facts in front of the U.S. attorney. We managed to raise all sorts of doubts about the credibility of their star witness, Joe Scarzone. Little by little, Fred and Patti made progress. The initial offer from the U.S. attorney's office started with a demand for an eight-year sentence. The prison time, though, kept shrinking as more and more facts were pushed across their desk.

Fred was finally able to discover why that office was so hell bent on driving this case so hard. It turns out that the U.S. attorney handling my case actually had despised Tom Connelly, and Fred seemed to think that somehow he saw me as an extension of his distain.

Apparently, Connelly was actually an ex-former U.S. attorney in Phoenix. And, he had quickly and quietly resigned from that office due to an investigation into his use of that title to benefit himself in outside personal business affairs. Then, since leaving that office, he was brought up in front of the bar for taking money from clients without doing any work. We also learned that Connelly had very few, if any, friends in those governmental agencies. This information was contrary to all he told me while he "represented" me.

It took a lot of work to overcome my position, but Fred was finally able to convince the U.S. attorney that Scarzone was not as innocent or truthful as they believed him to be. It was Fred who got them to realize that the loan Scarzone took out to buy my Mesa site was his own doing. That in addition to, the grouping of emails between my dad and me about the pending loan punched a lot of holes in Scarzone's story about my Dad being a shill.

But even with all this pushing and prodding by Fred and Patti, and the mounds of evidence in my favor, there was *no way* those charges were going to be dropped, not once that indictment had been issued; U.S. attorneys will *never* admit to mistakes; I believe they're far too prideful for that.

It would be career suicide for them.

So in late November of 2012, Fred and Patti called me to their office to discuss some important options on how to proceed. For this meeting, I asked my sister and parents to attend as well. I needed them there with me because they knew the facts. And, so Fred could speak to them in person as potential witnesses for my defense.

At the meeting, Fred told us that he got the U.S. attorney to agree to allow me to plea to one count of conspiracy to commit bank fraud, and that the count would have a sixty-month cap on it- that's *five years!* He also explained that the U.S. attorney now felt that Scarzone had lied to them, and that they were going to indict him for the lies and the fraudulent loan he took on the Mesa property.

Since the government would now be pursuing Scarzone, they would agree to give me a 5K-1 in my plea, if I agreed to "help them" in their efforts to indict and convict Scarzone. Fred explained that he felt that with this 5K-1 in place, and with him persuading the U.S. attorney to say a few good things to the sentencing judge, he felt he could get this to end with a 12-15 month prison sentence.

All I could think about when he said "12-15 months" was… WHY? Why would I sit for even one day for something I felt wasn't criminal? Something that I had lost a tremendous amount of money on? And, something in which there had never been any scheme to defraud?

I didn't think prison time was warranted, but that was Fred's number one recommendation. And Fred wasn't Connelly. He was smart, and competent. And I felt he had my best interests at heart.

Now for those not familiar with the 5K-1, it's a motion by the prosecutor asking a sentencing court to "depart downward," meaning a recommendation for a shorter range of sentences. The name comes from the authority granted a prosecutor to do this under section 5K1.1 of the United States Sentencing Guidelines.

Fred's second option presented to me was to not take the deal and take the government to trial. For this I'd need to get a lot of money together to defend my case. *If* I won, I'd walk. *But,* if I lost on *any* of the seven counts I was charged with, because in the eyes of the court I hadn't accepted responsibility and because the mandatory sentencing guidelines were now enhanced because of my prior, I was looking at big prison time. The not-so-rosy picture sounded something like this:

"Joe, we will go to trial. We will put on a big *show* at the trial, and with that show we'll most likely beat six out of the seven counts they charged you with, but your jury will be made up of twelve working class people; probably teachers and various lifelong employees.

"They will look at you, they will learn about the large amounts of money you made in your life, the homes you've lived in, the cars you drove, the boats, the plane, race horses, and so on. They will hear about your prior felony conviction on the ASU matter. They will know that your last name ends in a vowel, so I'm sure the U.S. attorney will try to somehow mention organized crime. When that happens, even if we put on an *amazing* show, that jury is going to think that just because of the things you've had in your life and the things you managed to do, that you had to do something very *wrong* to get them.

"Then Joe," he continued, "if that jury convicts you on even *one* of the seven counts at trial, without your accepting responsibility and pleading ahead of time, then you *will* be looking at mandatory minimums of one hundred and twenty months. Joe, that's ten *years!*"

I knew in my heart that Fred was right, which in my mind left me with just two choices to make. First, take the deal, then pray Fred could somehow convince the judge to grant a lenient sentence, which still probably meant I'd have to somehow deal with sitting over a year in prison for something I felt I didn't do.

Or for option number two, I could just leave the country, always looking over my shoulder, and not give this government a single day of my life locked up for what they said I did.

In the end I decided, after some nudging from my sister and parents (maybe because they just wanted this done), to go along with Fred. I told him that I would put my trust in him, and that I'd rely on him to get the best deal he could.

And so in late December 2012, I accepted the government's deal and pled guilty to a crime that looking back on, I'm unsure of what laws I broke. It was my only choice if I was to salvage anything of my life. When I walked out of the courtroom that day, I could practically *feel* that label of "Two-Time Convicted Felon" stenciled across my forehead.

Earlier in these writings, I tried to explain the stigma and guilt that being a *one*-time convicted felon filled me with, the depression and anxiety, so try to imagine if you will how many orders of magnitude worse it was now being saddled with the "two-time" label. Imagine the entire world pressing down on your chest trying to squeeze that last breath out of your lungs and you might have the beginnings of an idea how I felt. It goes beyond mere words.

About a week before Christmas of 2012 I left the courtroom, went home, and was alone for weeks. I hardly answered the phone, ordered delivery if I had to eat, and just laid in bed with the lights off, TV on but mostly unwatched.

My depression knew no bottom. The abyss was endless, dark and without remorse. I think the only time I left the house was to take Tracy and her daughter Peyton Christmas shopping to buy them and my own kids gifts the day before Christmas Eve with the little money I had.

It was good seeing them, and I tried to use that time to tell Tracy how I still felt about her. But inside I knew I was just a ticking time bomb waiting to explode. This was the worst and darkest period of my life by far. Those words may be the biggest understatement I could make…

Chapter Twenty-One:

Right Place at the Right Time

I left Tracy at the mall on December 23rd and went back to my house to lie alone in bed and sink into my dark and depressing world. Crazy thoughts swam through my mind like fleeting nightmares, almost-visions. I kept replaying my life in my mind, what I'd lost, whom I had let down, and how many times I'd failed. Oh, so many failures. With each one I remembered, I sunk deeper into despair. I didn't want to hear from anyone. I avoided my kids, my parents, and anyone who tried to contact me. The entire holiday season I separated myself from the world.

My depression was darker than the far reaches of outer space, darker than the middle of the ocean on a moonless night. So dark that I remember getting out of bed on New Year's Day, walking to my home office, and using the computer to search for different ways to commit suicide. As I read of the most common methods, I sat and played each one out in my mind, thinking about how it would feel and wondering how my family would find me after I did it.

I had hit rock bottom.

I knew in my heart that I could never hurt anyone else, but I truly thought that the only answer to my problems was to simply end my pain for good. I had convinced myself that taking control and ending my life would be the "noble" thing to do.

I made up my mind. But, first I needed to put my affairs in order so that whatever I did have left could be easily found and left to my kids. Then, the following week, I planned to man-up and end it.

It was the first Sunday after the first of the year. Knowing the plans I'd made to end it, I was so out of my mind that I actually believed I needed to go to church and try to somehow ask God for some forgiveness on what I was about to do.

Now, the church I'd normally go to was in Chandler, Arizona, about thirty minutes from my house, but that was the same church that Tracy attended. The last thing I wanted was to bump into her in the state I was in. I wanted her last memories of me to be good ones. So I decided to go to a church down the street that I'd heard about in Scottsdale. It was called "Impact Church" and that was the first time I'd ever been there.

I didn't think anyone would know me there, so I just tossed on a wrinkled T-shirt, pair of dirty shorts, flip-flops, and a baseball hat; in my mind set, I didn't care about looks. My plan was to walk into God's House, apologize to Him for messing up my life, and ask Him to forgive me for what I was about to do. Then leave and kill myself.

Service had started ten minutes earlier, so when I walked into the lobby that day there was only one man standing there. Mike McCann. I'd met Mike about fifteen years earlier through my brother, and we had hung out some together back in the Shammy Man days. But other than seeing him around town and giving quick hellos every now and then, I really hadn't talked to him in over five years. I knew him as "Cash", or Mikey Cash, so called because in his earlier days and when I'd first met him, he wasn't always on the right side of things, so seeing him there in a church lobby on a Sunday morning was a shocker.

From first glance I knew there was something different about him. First off, he was cleaning and helping as needed while the services were going on, donating his time to help. But beyond that, maybe he saw something in my face that told him that I was lost or in trouble, or maybe God put him there to save me, but when Mike saw me that day, he just would not leave my side. I had absolutely no intensions of telling him or anyone else a thing about what I was going through, but for reasons I still cannot understand, Mike kept asking me questions.

Cash was no stranger to the legal system himself, and after about half an hour of talking and having him pressing me, I spilled my guts.

"Okay, here it is. I was indicted again last year and a couple of weeks ago I pled guilty again in federal court. Cash, I'm looking at prison time again and it really has me in a funk. I'm messed up like you wouldn't believe. I... I've had it."

I never made it into church that day; we spoke for about an hour in that lobby and when services ended and the lobby started to fill, as Cash and I stood against the back wall still talking, I could tell that his eyes were searching for someone in the crowd to introduce me to.

In that mainly white crowd it wasn't too hard to find whom Cash wanted me to see: a six-foot four-inch good looking (that said just at his request) large-black man named Andre Wadsworth. Andre was one of the founders and the executive pastor of the Impact Church, not to mention former first round, third overall pick in the 1998 NFL draft, and up until the 2015 draft the highest drafted player to ever come out of Florida State University.

"Joe, this is Andre Wadsworth. He is the *most* sincere, honest, and genuine man that I have *ever* met. He saved me and changed my own life."

Cash was a street guy from New York who trusted very few, so I made sure to pay more attention when he made a comment like that.

I had briefly met Andre a few years earlier through another ex-Arizona Cardinal football player, but I never knew anything about him, the church, or what he stood for. Yet now, even with all the other people around us, the three of us talked for about twenty minutes about nothing of any real importance before Andre suggested we get together for lunch one day that week.

Thinking back to that now, it's really odd. Nothing was explicitly said to help me, and yet when I walked out of Impact Church that day I felt covered in love and concern from one man I knew as a street guy that I hadn't seen in over five years, and from another guy I'd just really talked to for the first time.

I walked into that church lobby that day lost and seeking God to forgive me for what I was going to do. Yet, I walked out of there about 90 minutes later, oddly comforted that something was happening.

Answers never come on *our* time, but they do come *in* time.

I drove back to my house a bit confused by my new feelings. After I got home I laid back in bed again, lights off, and crawled away into my depressed little world. At one point my phone rang with a number I didn't recognize so I let it go to voice mail; I doubt I would have answered it even if it were a number I knew. When I checked later it was Cash checking in on me. The message he left me lasted over a minute, but it was the concern in his voice that captured my attention, so I listened to it a few more times, trying to break it down.

Here was a guy whom just a few years earlier I would have never expected to see in church, let alone donating his time on a Sunday morning. His marriage was also doing *really* well; he and his wife had a daughter together and he was truly happy and content even though he was no longer making any real money since he'd lost everything when the economy collapsed.

Now he was simply working forty hours a week at a big company for an hourly wage. Cash told me that his peace and happiness came when he decided to just surrender all his issues to God, and that the understanding and peace learned for how that was possible was given to him from Andre.

This was a drastic change in Cash from when I'd known him... Well, it interested me enough to delay my dark plans and grab lunch with him and Andre.

The three of us met at a barbecue place just before noon, and stayed until almost four talking about life, family, business, my indictment, and other struggles. They shared perspectives from their own lives that helped me relate to the pain I was going through. It was a conversation without filter, the only thing I left unsaid was my plans to end it all; I was *way* too proud to show anyone that degree of weakness. It would just have been too embarrassing.

Even writing about those same thoughts right now fills me with emotions I have yet to completely conquer… but I'm working on it.

I knew that what I was planning to do was a weak, cowardly thing to even think about. I recalled a conversation I had with my dad when I was in high school after someone in my class killed himself.

"Joey," my dad told me, "no matter how bad things are or ever get, nothing is *ever* that bad."

That stuck with me. But, I was tired of being tired, and felt very ashamed. With all I was given in life. And, all the opportunities I'd had. I still managed to mess it all up. I just could not let go of the guilt from my wrongful actions while at the CBOT and the ASU scandal. Not to mention the prior and current felony convictions, along with breaking up of my family.

While I had no intention during that lunch to talk about my plans to kill myself, I guess the guilt I was carrying must have had its own way of speaking, because the two of them heard it clearly enough to come answering its call. There is just no other way to explain how, in my darkest of days, Cash and Andre were put in front of me at just the right time to rescue me.

I put my plans to end it all on hold for a few days, solely because those two saved me in ways I didn't think was remotely possible. I thought all hope was lost. But, I walked away from that four-hour lunch agreeing with them that I would attend next Sunday's services at Impact… and this time actually go inside.

I began to feel a little hope over the next few days, but I was still a mess. Cash called me a few times to check in, but mainly I just stayed home flipping through channels. But true to my word, I did go to services that Sunday. Cash met me in the lobby and introduced me to all kinds of people, as if he was actually proud to call himself my friend.

Proud to be *my* friend? Years of being beaten down, embarrassed, ashamed for what I had become, and yet he showed honest pride in our friendship. That helped me in more ways than he will ever know.

I finally attended the service. It was *perfect*; the energy of the congregation, the music, and the message all seemed to be just what I needed at that time. I left saying goodbyes to some people I'd just met, talked to Cash and Andre for a while, then allowed them to talk me into attending the men's group discussion on Wednesday night with a promise for dinner afterwards.

It was to be my first ever "Men's Group."

Sharing stories with a group of men, venting, and referencing Bible verses didn't appeal to me, not at all. I even tried to cancel Tuesday night by telling Cash that it just wasn't my scene. But he continued to press, assuring me that the group was nothing like that, so I caved and attended.

Andre headed the group and opened up the group for discussions on whatever guys might be struggling with. *That* was a real eye-opening experience. We were in North Scottsdale, so the room was filled with quite a few successful men, some of whom I knew by name, or at least I knew the companies they owned.

Some of the problems these men openly talked about really got my attention. Here were men I would have looked at and thought, "Wow, that guy really has it all together. Great family, successful business, money in the bank, everything." Yet it was shocking to see them break down about their struggles.

I had always believed that a truly successful and strong man must be stoic and *never* allow himself to show weakness to others. Even today I still somewhat lean toward this, but my time in that men's group helped me to see the need for a middle ground.

166

No matter what your stature in life, be it peasant or king, pauper or billionaire, know that *everyone* has struggles and issues. There was a saying I would often tell my kids and a few friends. The saying goes like this…

"You can tell the true character of a person by how he responds in the face of adversity."

I thought of that saying as I continued to listen to these men openly confront their struggles. In that moment, I had a much better understanding on what *true* character was. Everyone faces adversity, but what defines a person is *how* he or she reacts and faces it.

After the open discussion was over, Andre brought out a guest speaker. Bryan Schwartz was a retired middle linebacker for the Jacksonville Jaguars, and I swear I truly think he was sent there that day to tell me what I needed to hear. He talked for about an hour using passages from the Book of Romans, focusing on not persecuting yourself for past failures. In many different ways he repeated the theme that there is *no need* for you to carry those crosses on your shoulder or let them darken your heart. If you are a man of faith then know that Jesus carried that cross for us, so why weigh yourself down? Just move forward.

"Do *not* weigh yourself down with past guilt," he would say, "but simply do right by Him on a daily basis. Our faith forgives us for the past; you need to look only *forward*…"

Then he said a phrase that hit me like a baseball bat to the head.

"…The windshield in a car is much larger than the rear view mirror for a reason, and that reason is that the past is only a small part of your life; your focus should be on what lies ahead, for that is without end."

That comment stuck with me, and I walked out of Impact Church that night with feelings I'd never had before. For the first time in a *very* long time I literally had a spring in my step. I even called Tracy later that night, and she actually answered. When I told her that I'd just left the men's group at the church, I could hear the shock in her voice.

Tracy knew me as well as anyone and knew that I was *not* the type to ever talk openly to people about things in my life, and definitely *not* someone who ever showed or talked about faith or beliefs in God. I was always the one who listened in the room, then came up with a plan to act on my own. Hearing me speak about being in a men's group was something I knew would keep her thinking for quite some time.

Life is never over as long as there is hope, and the universe abounds with endless measures of hope. Hope is a funny thing to understand. Cling to hope by looking forward, not behind you. That's what I learned that night.

Thoughts of suicide were behind me now.

Chapter Twenty-Two:

9 Months to Get It All Back

It was now January of 2013. The court had taken my guilty plea and set my formal sentencing date for the end of October, which meant that I had about nine months to fix myself. Nine months; the same amount of time it takes for a baby to be born is the amount of time that I had to rebirth myself into a new life. Nine months to fix some strained relationships I held quite dear. Nine months to prepare financially for my kids while I was away. And just nine months to pursue the woman who held my heart in her hands.

Tracy.

I had quite the monumental task ahead of me, but this time was different. Before I would always hide behind my mask of what I thought others should see of me. Now, though, I was oddly comforted to know that I could let go, and throw away that mask. It had been the mask, after all, that had blinded me from what was actually in front of me.

Even with prison looming, I was excited to spend more time with my kids, and to show Tracy the true heart I'd always had but had been too embarrassed to show. I had many uphill battles ahead, but no longer would I be carrying the guilt of past mistakes.

For the freedom from guilt I learned that January, I will be forever grateful to Andre, Mikey Cash, and Impact Church. To this day I still tell Cash that he will never fully realize just how he saved me.

I kept in close contact with Andre, Cash, and a few other guys from Impact over the next few months as I submersed myself in my transformation. I was more focused on being a better father, on trying to under-promise and over-deliver; along the way I tried to show Tracy how I was changing and what she meant to me.

I thought I was making progress with Tracy. After all, we were meeting for dinner on occasion, talking on the phone several times a week, and some of these conversations were substantive. Everything was moving along, if slowly. Then in mid-July, I discovered that she was dating someone else. It was a long-distance relationship but it had been going on for several months.

She'd never told me. But then again, why would she? None of my business, after all. Personally, I was dating someone else too, and that was going pretty well. In fact, the girl I was dating was someone most guys would have killed for. A well-known model, with integrity and faith. But still it was very painful to discover that Tracy was in a relationship with someone else. So, I finally brought it up to her.

We talked about it for a couple hours on the phone one night, and I still believe that conversation was pivotal in showing her how I was changing. The old Joe would have screamed, then hung up abruptly to make a point. But now I never raised my voice, and even told her that I understood her choice. I only wished but one thing: that she would have told me earlier.

Her fortieth birthday was just two weeks away and I really wanted to make it special for her, but she told me on that call that she had already made plans with the other guy, and that he was flying into Arizona for a three-day stay.

That news was a body blow I never saw coming. Just a few years earlier she had done the nicest thing for me that anyone ever has; she threw me an amazing and very special fortieth birthday party in San Diego. Naturally, with her fortieth coming up I wanted to return the favor.

In the two weeks before her birthday, we did manage to go to dinner several times. On the night before the other guy was supposed to
arrive in Arizona, Tracy and I went to dinner and talked so long that
we closed down the restaurant, then spent a good half-hour in the
parking lot afterwards.

I begged her to call that guy and cancel her birthday plans, and I
want to think she almost considered doing it. But in the end she
wouldn't. I said goodbye to her that night in the parking lot and knew
that I had a *lot* of emotional pain coming my way the next few days.

Knowing that guy would be staying at her house, I ordered forty
long-stemmed roses delivered there with a *long* note attached to them.

Childish and petty? Yes, but it was a step up from my old ways,
which probably would have resulted in just pounding on him.

On Saturday night, her birthday, I hung out with some very trusted
friends. They took me out to dinner and tried to keep my mind busy
by playing cards at until midnight.

I tried to keep my mind on the card game, but inner demons kept
showing up. Little guys with pitchforks shaped like how I imagined
that other guy might look, stabbing into my brain. Such a very special
birthday and she was celebrating it with someone else. That was all I
could think of. I finally left my friend's house with them telling me to
go straight home and get some sleep.

I couldn't, of course. I ended up just driving around, stalking the
restaurant, club, and hotel where I knew Tracy, her family and friends,
and the guy were celebrating. I stayed out driving around past three in
the morning, and I'm just glad that I never actually bumped into them.

It was three-thirty in the morning when I finally got to where I was
staying. I tried to put my mind on hold and get some sleep, but it
didn't work. Nothing did. How do you sleep knowing that the person
you set your focus on is out celebrating with somebody else? So, I did
the one thing I had never done before, the one thing I never *thought* I
would do.

I dropped down to my knees and prayed.

With my whole heart and soul I prayed, my body actually shaking as I asked God for help and guidance. As strongly as I could, I focused on my kids, Tracy, my life, my family, and my future. I sobbed like a baby, submitting myself completely to His will, and for the first time ever in my life truly just asked for His help. Finally, my chips were all in on Him.

"Please God, just guide me on a path that if Tracy is meant to be my other half, let her see my heart and guide me to hers… Or failing that, if this is not in your plans, then comfort me so that I may cut the ties as needed. I just want what is best. Personally, I just want peace. Please…"

I had never really prayed in the past. Let alone ever prayed that way. Never ever came close to feeling what I felt. It was a powerful experience that I can only fail to put into words, and will probably never experience anything like it again. I exhausted myself with that effort and finally collapsed. I didn't wake up till eleven in the morning, then went to church. I was supposed to meet Tracy's dad, Brad for brunch afterwards.

The nighttime prayer did something to me and I was still thinking about it as I sat there in church. One of the church announcements that day was for a large-scale water baptism scheduled in a couple of weeks. Sitting there, I knew that was my next step. If I was going to walk the walk, I knew I had to be baptized.

Anyone who knows me knows that despite everything I've done and all my business accomplishments, I do not like public attention. And, I hate being in the spotlight. So naturally the very thought of others seeing me in public, at a church baptism, being viewed as a "bible thumper," really had me nervous. I mean *really* nervous.

After services ended I went back into Andre's office, shut the door, then sat down and started talking about… well, just random stuff. Finally, I came to the point.

"Dre, I need a favor from you. I was wondering if… if you would personally baptize me at the upcoming event."

A smile crossed my friend's face like the sun rising on a new day. He beamed with ethereal delight as he leaned forward and spoke.

"Joe, I wanted you on that list so badly, but I wanted the decision to be yours. So I didn't ask you; instead, I prayed about it. Of course I'll put you on the list. Man, I'm just really happy you made the decision."

I knew then I was making the right decision, even if I was shaking on the inside while doing it. When I left church to meet with Brad for brunch, I knew that for the first time in a very long while I had actually made a *good* life choice. Me! The King of Wrong Choices, finally doing something right.

I met with Brad and we ordered food and started talking about a lot of things. He told me some of the details of the previous night's birthday dinner and Tracy's "new guy," and I in return told him about the new things going on with me. Then he told me about the birthday dinner the night before.

"Tracy had a great time," he said. "Her and the other guy get along pretty well, but there was something missing. There was no spark between them, no gleam in her eyes. Joe, she doesn't love him, not really."

I thought, is that hope I feel? Can it truly be?

"Joe, I urge you: keep fighting for her. The two of you are perfect for each other."

I worked my mouth but no words came out. I was still pondering the moment when my cell phone rang. I looked down to see who it was and my eyes nearly bugged out.

"It's Tracy! I… have to take this."

I walked away from the table and took the call. She called me the moment she'd dropped the other guy at the airport. It *must* have been a sign and I was going for it.

"Tracy," I finally said, "I've decided to be baptized."

"What? Baptized?"

"Yes. I've given it a lot of thought and decided I need to do this. I also... It's very important to me that you be there with me."

I could hear the shock in her silence. She knew me, and yet this was something different.

"Well, yes, I guess. Of course I'll be there."

The conversation drifted. Best conversation I had that entire day, or in a long time before that, until we came to the subject of her birthday.

"Look, I know it'll be a week late, but let me take you out next Saturday for your birthday. We'll spend all day just celebrating your fortieth. How does that sound?"

"It sounds like a date."

The following Saturday I picked her up at ten in the morning and took her shopping at two great outdoor malls in Scottsdale. Tracy rarely spent money on herself; she always felt that she had to be a wise steward with her earnings to protect and provide for her daughter.

I had made a few dollars a couple months earlier putting together a sale of a shopping center on the west side of Phoenix, so I was able to plan something nice. For this day, however, I wanted Tracy to focus on herself. To just carelessly buy things she wanted or just because they made her smile. For hours we shopped like that, breaking only for a great lunch, with a few drinks.

I set up dinner for us in a private section of a great restaurant called Bourbon Steak inside the Princess Hotel in North Scottsdale, with the two of us talking over a *twelve* course meal. Each course was personally selected by the chef. There were also a couple bottles of excellent wine.

I gave her a card that night, with a long handwritten note, then asked the waiter to take a picture of us together. Tracy looked absolutely beautiful, like an angel with the stars in her eyes.

That picture will always be my favorite one of us together, and will always symbolize a couple of things to me. First, despite the past issues I'd endured, and the status of my criminal case, for the first time in my entire life I was doing things right.

The second thing was of Tracy herself. I knew her, her body language, her smile, how she reacts to things, and after spending that day together and the time we enjoyed, I knew one thing for certain, and that made the whole world brighter.

I had Tracy back.

Tracy and I – The night I got her back

The next weekend was my baptism, and the church service was packed. All three of my kids were there, along with my ex-wife, a few treasured friends, and of course Tracy. It really melted my heart to see my friends watching me make this commitment, but it was Tracy's tears of joy that showed me all I ever needed to know about what we had together. Much like the Grinch, my heart grew three sizes that day.

My buddy Andre baptized me in front of a full house. I introduced Tracy to my Impact family. She was shocked by the amount of people who cared and how truly happy these people were with my baptism. She saw the change in me, and the true heart I'd long been ashamed to show.

Baptized by Andre at Impact Church

Things felt different after the baptism. My conversations with Tracy had more levity to them, but great meaning as well. We made plans for a weekend getaway to Del Mar, California a couple of weeks down the road. Until then, she had some conflicts in her schedule, and since

I wasn't working until my sentencing, I killed time by flying back and forth to Vegas to see my family and make the occasional bet on a football game. My hobby I guess.

There was a three-week period, with trips to Vegas, during which I could do *no wrong*. Even though I wasn't betting all that big, I did nothing but pick football winners, and in most cases they'd win in very unusual ways. I was convinced that this winning streak was because of my baptism, that somehow the waters had washed all my sins away and allowed me to go on this winning streak.

I called Andre all the time while I was in Vegas during most of the games to tell him that I wanted to do this "baptism thing" every couple of weeks, and that I was going to put him on retainer as my "personal dunker" so the winning streak wouldn't be compromised. I even tithed to the church off my winnings. That was new for me. But while winning a few games and making some bucks was fun and made me smile, it was my kids, Tracy, and my upcoming sentencing that had my *full* attention.

I scheduled the Del Mar trip for the last week of September, and I went *all out*. I started by flying first class, then took a limo for all ground travel. I booked us a suite at one of the best resorts in Southern California, The Grand Del Mar. I lined up spa appointments, made reservations to restaurants I knew were tough to get into, and arranged a shopping trip in the downtown area of one of our favorite cities, La Jolla, California.

The perfect weekend at the perfect time.

As it turned out, there was something else going on where we were staying. LeBron James was having his own surprise wedding on the property that same weekend, so we were bumping into the likes of Jay-Z, Beyonce, Pat Riley, Dwayne Wade, and other notables. Heck, I spent thirty minutes in the sauna chatting with Dwayne Wade. He was a Chicago kid as well, so we really hit it off. And no, I didn't get him to shave points.

It was official: Tracy and I were back together. But I didn't just want the boyfriend-girlfriend label, not this time around. The sentencing was coming up in four weeks, and Tracy and I had already been separated for the past year, so I wanted to tell the kids that we were getting back together.

I sat down with my kids and told each of them about the mistakes I'd made in the past with Tracy and how I'd worked *very* hard to fix them and, to get her back. I even told my ex-wife, and to her credit she told me that the kids had actually missed Tracy.

So with all the blessings in place from the people I cared about, Tracy and I decided to tell her daughter, Peyton. Just as I'd hoped, she too was happy we were getting back together. Things were moving forward.

Before the sentencing, though, I wanted one more trip with Tracy, and this time we decided to bring Peyton along. The second week of October we flew into Vegas for a weekend stay, but I had in mind something more.

The three of us arrived that Friday and got a suite at the Bellagio Hotel. I made spa appointments for all of us, got tickets to see a show each night, and ate at some Vegas's best restaurants. We even managed to do some shopping. But my plan involved something a bit more.

I'd spent the previous two weeks designing a ring, and having it made. I knew I was going to give it to her but didn't know how. With all the shopping we'd done that weekend, she was able to buy most of what she wanted, but there was still a Fendi purse she had her eyes on.

It was the morning we were supposed to leave Las Vegas and I was running out of time. I bought the purse and put the ring inside of the beautiful box the purse came in, then after breakfast in our suite, as the bellhop was coming up to the room for our bags, I presented the wrapped box.

"Tracy, I know you had your eye on this."

"The Fendi purse," she gasped. "Joe..."

"Try it on."

Peyton was in the room as Tracy unwrapped the box. Peyton dashed over when her mother gasped. By that time, however, I had dropped down to one knee.

"Tracy, you know I love you. Will you marry me?"

A nod at first as tears streamed down her face, before Tracy finally managed that one word I wanted to hear.

"Yes!"...

She was in my arms a second later, with Peyton acting as our cheering section. When we got into the waiting limo she had the ring on her finger. For the entire flight back to Scottsdale, we alternated between looking at the ring and each other. We arrived in Arizona in time to see my "little brother" Ryan marry his beautiful bride Shernaz, and perhaps get a glimpse of what was in store for us.

I will always remember that day, the day that erased many of the dark places in my soul and replaced them with a little inner light.

Chapter Twenty-Three:

Sentenced...Again

I was engaged! I had Tracy back and now I could focus all my efforts towards my sentencing in two weeks. I managed to get about two hundred people to write letters of reference to the judge, worked on a prepared speech, and lined up a few people to speak on my behalf at the sentencing. I think that with the situation we faced, my attorneys and I did the best that we possibly could to prepare. The rest was left to God and faith.

On the day of the sentencing Tracy and I drove to the federal courthouse together, many others showed up to support me. In fact, we nearly filled all the seats on my side of the room. I walked into the courtroom thinking a worst-case scenario of fifteen months, and my attorneys thought that under a year was possible. They even suggested that if favorable comments were to be made by the U.S. attorney as promised, that house arrest or probation could still be an option.

I braced myself for what I thought was the worst while trying to wrap my head around sitting somewhere alone, away from my family for a year and half. Nervous? Yes, but now I had a clear mind, focused on the future, with Tracy by my side.

The hearing went as the attorneys said it would. Fred said many nice things about me and the changes I'd made in my life. Then my friends spoke on my behalf. David Beckham, Shirl Zeleznak, and Andre Wadsworth all spoke of their interactions with me.

Then I gave a five-minute speech about the changes I'd made and the guilt I'd carried for years because of the 1994 ASU conviction. At that point, all things seemed to be going pretty well, and the judge even pointed out that he was impressed by the support of the people in attendance and the many letters he received from others.

Then came the U.S. attorney. This was the *same* guy who told us he now understood the events and that he would "let the judge know" at my sentencing the beneficial things I'd done.

However, he decided to use that stage as a platform to tell the judge and the mass of people I had in the courtroom all about the details of the other six counts the government had charged me with but were *not* proven and I didn't agree to plea on.

He managed to misrepresent to the judge about my timely acceptance of responsibility for the one count I did plead guilty on, as well as botch a few other details about my case. In my view, he used that opportunity to grandstand for his own personal agenda. I was enraged!

Enraged over how scarce the truth seems to be held in our system. Enraged that I had to stand there and allow someone to misrepresent details about my actions with no counter defense. And more enraged watching my attorneys not object to this man's words?

I was about to personally interrupt and attempt to tell the judge what was being said was not accurate. But my attorney grabbed my arm and whispered in my ear to relax. Right then, I knew what was coming.

That day, all was confirmed to me that in the federal criminal system, it didn't matter how right you were, or what rules you had played by. At that moment, in that courtroom, with my freedom waiving in the wind, it was simply my felony label against the U.S. attorney's spoken words. All I could do was sit back and take the blows.

Sure enough, after the U.S. attorney spoke, the judge lectured for almost five minutes before he pronounced his sentence. He spoke about how I had obviously *not* learned my lesson from the fifteen-month sentence twenty years earlier, and spoke about how I had *not* accepted timely responsibility on the matter the government had charged me with.

All of which was I felt were simply not true.

He told me that my actions had caused the bank to lose money and restricted it from lending money to others. To me, that seemed like a selective version of the truth. The judge's entire lecture to me basically echoed the speech the U.S. attorney had made to the court.

After all, when you dissect the dynamics of a federal courtroom, the U.S. attorneys and federal judges work together and see each other on multiple cases. They have personal relationships in place. With that, and the U.S attorneys close involvement bringing the charges, judges rely on those spoken words for their final judgements.

Those judgements are indeed final. Because federal judges are appointed by the presidents and *no one* can fire them; no one has more judicial power.

At that time, as I stood awaiting my fate, I was simply the prior-convicted felon who had to be held accountable. Details and reasons didn't matter.

It became very clear the direction the judge was going with me. No matter what we said, did, or gave to the judge that day, my sentence had been pre-determined even before I stepped into that courtroom.

The judge sentenced me to *thirty* months in a federal prison and a $2.9 million dollar fine. All I could do when I heard this was lower my head while many in the courtroom behind me broke into tears. Fred and Patti assured me that they would still fight and press hard to correct the U.S. attorney's misrepresentations spoken that day in the courtroom, but I knew they were just trying to comfort me.

The case was *over*. I was sentenced. The tactics used to get their victory no longer mattered to me; all that mattered was making sure that Tracy and the kids were provided for while I went away.

Tracy took it really hard, crying uncontrollably. She knew how I had been changing my life, as well as the details of events that I'd been sentenced on, so it hurt her as much as a physical blow.

"It's okay," I told her as I wrapped my arms around her. "We're only going to be stronger because of this."

She returned my hug, then pulled back to look me in the face. Her eyes were filled with tears. And said something I wish could be said under far better circumstances.

"Joe," she said, "before you have to leave, let's get married."

Chapter Twenty-Four:

A Little Happiness... Before The Storm

I was given a few months to surrender myself into federal custody. Time to get some family matters in place and to deal with all the many personal things that needed to be addressed... which included telling my children what was going on. I was going to be gone for two and a half years and there was no dancing around that; they had to know, and that would be a *big* challenge.

This wasn't like the first time I went away when my girls were four and five years old. They were old enough now that they had to know the truth. My little guy was just five, so the plan was to simply tell him that I had to go away to work on something.

There was a lot to do, not the least of which was to plan a wedding! And, I had to make this absolutely the best wedding I could.

We'd always talked about getting married on a beach or near water, so with the help of my buddy Andre, we were able to reserve the day after Thanksgiving at an incredible resort called Pelican Hill in Newport Beach, California. Picture something with a high-end Mediterranean flare rubbing elbows with the Pacific Ocean. That's Pelican Hill.

To accomplish what we did, in the style it happened in just *three* weeks was nothing short of incredible. I hired one of the best wedding planners I could find in southern California.

That wedding planner was a true pro. All I had to do was just sit back and let Tracy pick out everything she wanted.

The ceremony was held on an outdoor rotunda overlooking the ocean. For Tracy and me it was all about *us,* the kids, and a small group of friends. Peyton walked Tracy down the aisle, while my two girls, Gianna and Raina, were bridesmaids; my son was Matteo the ring bearer. How the kids looked that day, along with the pictures and memories made can't be described in words. It was near perfection, a postcard in my mind that will *never* be erased.

Me, Tracy, and the kids – Wedding day

The only thing that could have made the day more perfect was if my parents had been able to attend. My dad was battling cancer once again and fighting through his chemotherapy, and couldn't make the trip.

We would have loved a honeymoon, but there was just no time for one. I had thirty days of freedom remaining to prepare things financially for my family. And I still had to sit down with each of the kids and explain to them how I was going away for a while.

Oh, and on top of all that, my five-year-old son had to have heart surgery for a hole doctors had found in his heart a few months earlier. Each of those remaining days was pure chaos.

First I sat down with my oldest daughter, Gianna. We'd always had a special relationship, and she is just a pure soul with an amazing heart. We'd spent a lot of time together the previous couple of years touring colleges together. She's wickedly smart, with dreams of practicing medicine when she graduates. I can't tell you how proud I am of her.

I sat her down on a Sunday after church to tell her everything, and boy was it painful. The tears started flowing from the get-go. That absolutely crushed me; my daughter should be smiling, not crying. Then she began to process the amount of time I'd be gone and hit me up with a few questions.

"So, you won't be here for my senior prom?" she asked.

"So, you're going to miss my high school graduation?"

"You are not going to be here when I leave for college next year?"

I had to answer no to all three.

Then I told her about the crime I was charged with, and that the *only* reason I'd pled guilty was so I could put all this behind me and get back to her and her siblings as soon as possible. I told her that if I was to fight the case and lost, I would have been gone for a decade.

There was no real need to explain the judicial system to her, although I think she got that picture clearly on her own.

I wanted to let her know that even though I would not be around every day that I would still be available via phone or email. And, yes, prison has email.

A couple of days later it was my turn to talk with my next daughter, Raina. She is a *very* strong-willed person and because we are both so much alike, sometimes we have a difficult time communicating. Right or wrong, she'll never back down and she has the *same* fight in her heart that I do. Now Raina is no intellectual slug. She excels in school, made the National Honor Society, works hard at an after-school job, saves her money, and *loves* the theater. I know she'll surprise everyone with what she accomplishes in life.

I anticipated a short conversation. Boy, was I wrong. I spoke for about twenty minutes, and when I was done, I asked her how she felt about it all.

She looked me in a way that I will *never* forget and said. "I'm grateful".

Now, Raina and I sometimes clash heads because we are both so stubborn, so when she said that, I actually wondered to myself if she was grateful that I was going away for thirty months.

"Raina, what… what do you mean by that? How are you grateful?" I asked.

She then stared me dead in the eye. "I'm grateful to have a father that would do what you did so we could have a better life."

I nearly lost it.

That *one* moment made everything I did make sense. Raina was- and *still* is- the only one in my entire family who came close to saying thank you. If she can just somehow learn from the many mistakes I've made in my life, then there will be *no* stopping her.

Raina, if you're reading this, I pray that these writings will help you choose better paths that I did.

Tracy and I decided to tell Peyton together. "P" just makes me smile every time I see her. She loves school, applies herself in all things, loves her friends, loves to dance, and loves her family. Over the years the two of us have formed an incredible bond. No matter what happened between her Mom and me, she's always shown me unconditional love. A long time ago she earned a place in my heart as my third daughter, so marrying her mom only made it official.

We explained the details to P, and that I would be going away for a while. It was important to both Tracy and me that P knew I would be safe, and that she could see and talk to me whenever she wanted. I told her that I would need her help taking care of her mom, and how I was depending on her to come through for me. P then asked her questions, but in the end the only thing she focused on was that we were all together now, as a family.

When it came to my five-year-old son Matteo, we decided he was too young to process it all. To him "jail" was a *really* bad thing that had something to do with the Teenage Mutant Ninja Turtles' way of life. Missing his little-boy growing years would be a struggle, but time at that age is meaningless. I knew when I got home, he would be my focus.

With Tracy as my wife, some money set aside from winning football weeks in Vegas and a few real estate deals I was able to get paid on, I knew I could provide for the needs of all while I was away. That was vital to my peace of mind.

I felt good knowing that my kids now knew the details behind what their father did so they wouldn't be embarrassed, I had most of the details needed in place to go sit in prison for two and a half years of my life. Just one detail remaining.

Matteo's heart surgery.

A few months earlier, three different cardiology groups diagnosed Matteo with a quarter sized hole in one of the chambers of his heart, causing him to lose about twenty to twenty-five percent of his normal blood flow. While it wasn't life threatening, all three groups strongly advised he have the operation now, so that later in life it wouldn't be a concern.

The operation was scheduled for a week before I was to leave, at Children's Memorial Hospital in Phoenix. We arrived there at six in the morning and they prepped him for surgery. Seeing your five-year-old being put to sleep for heart surgery is a sight I would not wish on any parent. Watching as he was wheeled to the operating room was a painful sight, and waiting was excruciating.

A couple hours after they took him back for surgery, the doctor came out to the visiting room. He said he wanted to talk to the parents alone, so we walked into a back room with him and he closed the door.

"I'm not sure what to say" He said…

Those first words of his made my heart sink into my stomach. But then he quickly amended himself.

"No wait, it's not what you think. Before we started the procedure, we put a camera down his throat just to see the *exact* size of the hole again. But what we ended up seeing… Well,…The hole is no longer there. It seems like over the last few months, the hole fixed *itself*. I just couldn't believe it, so we called in other doctors to verify it. And, they all said the same thing."

"Wait," I began, "You mean… he's okay?"

Tears came to my eyes as he nodded in the affirmative.

"We had a ton of people praying," I told him.

He looked at me with almost a cold, callous look. One that they must somehow teach these guys in medical school and said.

"Well, you can believe in miracles and other things you may want to believe in," he said, "but all I can tell you is that your son *had* a hole in his heart a few months ago, and now it's no longer there."

I knew this was a true miracle given to us that day. And, that this was the best going-away present that God or anyone could ever give me.

By far the best gift ever.

With Matteo's health no longer a stress, my checklist grew much smaller. In fact, there was just one thing left for me to suck up and do, so two days before I was supposed to surrender into custody, I flew to Vegas to say goodbye to my parents.

Even with the bad feelings I still harbored towards them with not standing tall for me on the second set of charges, and how they'd invited the FBI into their home and made the comments they made. I still loved my parents.

I needed to try to let go and forgive my thoughts that they and my family seemed to turn their backs to me in my dire time of need. I knew they didn't attend the baptism, the sentencing, or the wedding. But they were still my parents. I was raised with that respect. Knowing we are all flawed, I needed to forgive.

So I made the trip. Maybe it's an Italian thing. Or, just the way I'm wired. But when something is bothering me and on my mind, I just have to say it. Then usually after it's said, I tend to forget what I was upset about in the first place.

With that, I spent a couple hours with my folks. And, said a few things I felt needed to be said. I apologized for the many mistakes I had made in my life and how it shamed them. I knew I could not blame them for turning their backs on me, but also felt compelled to share with them how it felt.

I told them about how I felt kicked to the curb by them and all in our family. I told them my thoughts that when things were good, everyone was on board for the ride. But when I needed them, especially on details they were involved with, they all looked the other way. I raised my voice some at times, and they had little to respond with. But, at least I openly said what I felt. Our time together ended well. Because in the end, even with feelings hurt, or disappointments had from others. We are a family. And, in our family, there is a strong underlying love for each other.

They drove me back to the airport. When we got there, my mom stayed in the car. As sick as my Dad was, he put the car in park and walked me to the door. I could see the pain in his eyes as he walked towards me. He came up to me and after a pause, he gave me a hug, the tightest hug we ever shared. The hug lasted longer in my heart than I deserved and it remains there to this day.

As I said good-bye, then turned to walk away to the airport, all I could do was wipe away the tears from my eyes. My father will always be my hero. I love you, Dad.

The next day was Super Bowl Sunday, the day before I had to leave. I spent the entire day with Tracy, the kids, and a few friends. We went to church together, grabbed lunch, and watched the game together. There were lots of tearful goodbyes that night with the kids, then the next morning with Tracy. But it had to happen.

There was no easy ways to leave.

I drove myself to Impact Church to meet Andre and a few friends at eight in the morning for a few more goodbyes.

Andre then drove me to the U.S. Marshall's office to self-surrender for my thirty-month stay in federal prison. Thirty months… away from Life, Family, and Tracy. Oh, the weight of those thoughts.

It's odd how people think that the actual prison time is the tough part of an ordeal like this. I can tell you that it's far tougher being investigated for years, working on your case, fighting for your innocence, being indicted, awaiting sentencing, and then being sentenced.

When the time comes to leave for prison, even though you're going to be away from those you love, you almost feel like a weight has been lifted off your back. In the end going away and sitting in prison might just be the easy part.

Chapter Twenty-Five:

Prison, the Second Time Around

It had been almost fifteen years since I'd been in the prison system, during which time I'd managed to forget how rude, cruel, and callous it was. It took just a few minutes into my surrender, for it all to come flooding back. Once you're an inmate, you cease being a person and become just a number. You are treated like an enemy. You're told what to do, when to do it, and how to do it.

Most of the people working in a prison probably had their lunch money stolen from them when they were kids. Their new-found authority over others gives them a chance for payback. Day one they set the tone. It was *hell*.

Strip searches, handcuffs, leg shackles, and one five-foot by seven-foot holding cell after another. Guards who look at you and treat you with distain. Armed prison transport bus after bus while we made our way to a detention holding center.

The detention holding center facility was where I was fully processed, and that was one rough ride. In the prison world they call it "diesel therapy." Riding a caged prison transport bus with shackled arms and legs while the bus is filled with all types of criminals makes you wish you had eyes behind your head. Some of the guys on that transport bus had some serious life issues.

I finally made it to the detention center in Florence, Arizona at around 7 p.m. that night, along with five or six hundred other inmates, all waiting processing. I was nearly the *only* white guy there; most of the rest were illegal immigrants between the ages of 18 to 30, and they all seemed to smell like the back end of a mule.

Most were picked up at the border crossing over with drugs or other criminal intent, and all were wearing the same clothes they had on them when they were caught. Same clothes, no showers for days, after being picked up in the middle of the desert. I'll let you imagine the awful smell.

Oddly enough, though, most of them seemed happy to be there. I guess having three meals a day and a place to sleep was an upgrade. From about eight to two in the morning that night I sat with a hundred and twelve of the foulest smelling guys you could imagine in a holding cell that had the words "Maximum Capacity of 48" painted on the wall.

And yes, I actually counted the number of people in the cell with me. What else was I supposed to do to take my mind off the smell?

It was two in the morning when I finally got moving through the processing route. When I got to the medical part of the processing, I had an English-speaking male nurse examining me. It seemed the nurse was happy to see a white dude, and get to speak English.

So, he said to me… "Are you doing OK?"…

"Other than being sick from the smell of others," I answered "I'm alright."

"Well," he said as he tapped me on the leg, "I'll help you."

I actually thought that maybe I'd finally caught a break; maybe he took pity on me and would put me up in a nice spot. Maybe this guy was actually going to help me.

Nope, not even close. The nurse had the guards escort me into medical isolation, where I was put in a 5x7 box that was bright as can be: all white cinder block, with no windows and a thick metal door. There was nothing but a six-foot piece of sheet metal to lie down on, a metal sink, and a metal toilet.

The room had a panic/call button on the wall. And, 20 minutes into me being in there, pacing around from wall to wall, I pressed it. Thank God no one answered. Looking back now, if they had, I probably would have been in straightjacket. I did all I could to attempt to calm down. I took my shirt off and rinsed it in water from the sink. Laid on the sheet metal with the wet shirt over my head. And, read the prison manual they gave me in Spanish. I know little-to-no Spanish, but that managed to calm my mind anyway.

The fluorescent light overhead was *always* on. Hearing that thick metal door close with the sound of finality was something I will always remember. I was in that room for four *days* of isolation. Four days of panic attacks and anxiety, four days of alternating hot or cold slop tossed onto a Styrofoam tray and slid through a small opening in the door three times a day.

I've always been a fan of alone-time, but this was carrying things rather far.

After my fourth day a nurse came in and seemed to take pity on me. That afternoon I was moved into a three-man 7x9 foot cell in a pod with a hundred other guys. We were on lock-down in that cell for 18 hours a day. Neither one of my "cellies" spoke a lick of English and I was the *only* white guy in the pod. Needless to say, this meant that any extras or favors that came in the area never went in my direction.

If it wasn't for the few thirty-minute visits I had from Andre and Ryan, I'm not sure how I would have kept my sanity. It was about a month and a half in that detention center when I was called out at midnight to be transported to the federal prison where I would spend the rest of my time. As bad as those first 45 days had been, I'm a bit grateful for the experience. Grateful, because although I'd seen that type of prison life in the movies, until actually experiencing it myself I would have never known such a thing was real. Up until that time, I thought that prison was like the time I'd spent 15 years earlier at Nellis in Las Vegas.

The bulk of the next day was spent traveling via the Bureau of Prisons and some U.S. Marshals. I rode handcuffed and leg shackled on a secured bus with armed guards, and several other inmates.

There were many stops at other prisons to drop people off along the way. The bus was down to only a handful of guys left when we stopped at a U.S Penitentiary –"USP". USP's are high security prisons. With razor wire, guard towers, and house the worse of the worse in the criminal world. With the armed guards searching all of us that remained and barking orders, we were all told to get off the bus and form a line. In that line we were directed to all start walking towards the prison intake section.

As "hard" as I attempted to be on the outside, I can tell you that fear devoured my insides. The thought of spending 30 months in this maximum security prison looking over my shoulder 24/7 for pure survival made me numb. I thought to myself, "This has to be a mistake. I don't belong here. Someone messed up the paperwork somewhere".

After our line was about 20 feet from going inside the intake office, one of the guards yelled out "Gagliano and Madrid, back on the bus". Even though I was still going to a prison, I knew I wasn't going to be at the USP. I was actually oddly happy. But, couldn't show it. I had to show strength. Weakness would make me seem like prey to others.

After that, and many hours of waiting in various other holding cells, I finally made it to what would be my new home, a federal prison camp in Tucson, Arizona.

As I looked around, there were no prison bars anywhere, no fences or walls around the property, no cells for inmates. Just a big building with bunk beds where over a hundred and fifty guys stayed on the honor system not to walk away and to self-surrender each night.

There were quite a few guards walking around the property, and a few things that were known to absolutely get you tossed out of there and put behind "the wall," but overall, as long as you didn't cause trouble, it was the best worst place to be.

Mainly two types of people are at these camps: white collar or drug cases. Most of the white-collar crimes criminals got caught up in the world's financial collapse of 2008, while the drug offenders were stuck serving ridiculous amounts of time for a non-violent first-time offense because of Ronald Reagan's "War on Drugs," and its mandatory sentencing laws.

In most of the cases, the government had used an incredible word that's in their arsenal, and that word is "conspiracy". When the government wants to make a case stick, if there is *any* doubt if they can get a conviction, they have the luxury of calling something a "conspiracy."

Conspiracy or not, I now sit in this federal prison with ample time to write the story of my life, and reflect on the things I did and the choices I've made. I'm happy that I didn't tell you my story in 2000 when the ASU hype was highest, and when crazy amounts of money were offered to me. At that time, my perspective on life was very different. If I had told a story, it would have been one that glamorized an ugly situation.

My daily sanity while here comes from looking forward to weekend visitors. A grouping of a trusted circle of friends always prioritized Saturdays and Sundays to make sure I am never alone.

They would make the 90 minute plus trip to see me, sitting on plastic chairs or concrete benches, while together we ate from vending machines. I wore my green prison gear, and they did their best to fill me in on the outside world. They did this just to make sure I felt loved. And, to continue to fill me with hope.

Here is a picture one Saturday of me, Andre, Mikey Cash, and a buddy Mark Burns. Makes me laugh looking at it. With the tree in the background and my green outfit, it almost looks like they took a picture with a landscaper.

Mikey Cash - Mark Burns - Me - Andre - Visiting me in prison

Maybe its maturity, or just personal progress made via my life's journeys, but now, I have two different perspectives.

The first perspective is one of anger. Anger that is directed at myself and myself alone. Anger because I know I didn't do what they claimed I did, yet I had to bow down and plead for mercy mainly because of the foolish choice I *had* made 20 years earlier, a choice for which I thought I'd already paid my debt.

Anger at myself because for years I didn't know who I was or whom I needed to please. That confusion had me struggling with life choices. It was never about right or wrong. Because I knew the difference. No, for me it was about better understanding faith and knowing that integrity should *never* be compromised.

Anger at myself because I regret that I never had confidence in my faith and integrity. At the age of 45, my life finally began to take shape when I learned I only had to perform for an audience of *one*. It just really stinks that I had to learn this lesson through so much pain and so many wasted blessings.

My other perspective is one of peace. Peace in the knowledge that wisdom does come through experience and age. Peace in knowing my purpose on this earth is just starting…that I have a new and exciting life ahead where I can make better decisions and create much better outcomes for myself, my family and the world.

Now, the way I break down life is that if I can keep my audience of *ONE* happy then all the rest of the things I could possibly stress over will fall into place.

Chapter Twenty-Six:

The Rear View Mirror…

As I sit in federal prison to write this and reflect on why God and the government chose this path for me, some recurring thoughts kept popping up in my head.

Accountability for my early life actions seems to be the main thought I keep focus on. The early life choices I made allowed me to wrongly think that grey areas were acceptable spaces to play in.

At first, those simple grey areas seemed innocent enough. Over time, the decisions I made, small grains of sand at the time, grew into mountains of pain and suffering. With those moral mountains in front of me, I was forced to be held accountable for actions that surely would have gone unnoticed if not for my questionable past.

As for why God chose this path for me. In my mind it's pretty simple. He knew I could handle it. And, in handling it, He knew I could make a difference along the way via using my voice as a platform to help others who may be struggling with the same life choices as I had.

Most of us count on a level playing field. Don't kid yourself; it doesn't exist. I was *so* naïve and a glutton for punishment that I actually believed in the honor of others to do as they said they would. That's another life lesson learned. As my buddy Andre says, everyone will disappoint and let you down one time or another. The faster one accepts that, the quicker you'll take responsibility for your own life.

So now, because of my life choices made, I'm left to sit here in prison and hope the days pass quickly.

As much as I wish for accountability, and a less selective and more equal approach to criminal prosecution, I blame *no one* for the peaks and valleys in my life but *myself*. I had everything I needed to succeed in life; a good childhood, attentive and caring parents, and all the opportunities for education that I could wish for. Yet somewhere along the line I made a choice to veer off in a different direction.

When I first thought of putting my life to pen and paper I had a couple of goals. The first was *not* to dive into truly private and personal matters. The second was to try to show that *every* choice we decide on in our lives creates a new path to follow. Any given choice may seem harmless at the time it's made, but sooner or later you will see its consequences.

Any choice we make needs to be solely based on whether it's right or wrong. Your choice must please an audience of *One*. You must be able to stand proud of your decision.

My hope is that because of the painful lessons I've learned my kids can focus on their own life choices. With our oldest now 19 and the youngest 7, the choices and peer pressures they'll face will put their values to a strong test. I personally failed on many of my early life choices. I can tell my kids about those failures over and over, but I hope by reading this, it will hit home.

My poor life choices started when I failed to be held accountable for the first big investment made in me with Joey's Place.

From there it was one bad choice after another.

I gave into peer pressure and tossed my integrity away for the first time when I knowingly fixed the Super Bowl squares on the trading floor of the CBOT.

I followed that up by making an unethical choice when I created fraudulent revenue dialing 900 numbers on random phones for Wizard Sports.

I chased after greed when I simply could have given my brother's college roommate a few sports picks. Instead, I pushed for him to open an account for me so that I could selfishly reap the rewards.

I bribed college basketball players that were easy victims, while tarnishing college athletics just for more greed and personal gains.

I made a very poor choice when I refused to listen to professional advisors, and partnered up with Reggie Fowler. Doing this because I was layered in guilt from prior choices already made.

I allowed the SBA loan documents to get removed from a title company so I could close an SBA loan without a proper power of attorney in place.

And, I made an exceedingly poor choice in the attorney I selected during an investigation I was the target of.

I can look back now at *all* of these major life choices and realize that for all of them- **every single last one**- I knew absolutely at the time the choice was being made, that the choice I was making was *WRONG*....

And yet, even with that knowledge, and that voice inside telling me that it was wrong, I still continued to push forward with that choice. All in the name of instant gratification. And, in *every* choice, I suffered a great consequence.

There is little I can do about the past now except learn from the mistakes. As Bryan Schwartz said in that first men's group sermon I attended,

"The rear view mirror is smaller than the windshield for a reason, and that reason is for us to focus on what lies ahead."

As I sit in federal prison with still over a year left on my sentence, I am at an odd peace with my life. I look forward to the challenges that await. Despite the struggles and obstacles I've faced, I know without any doubt that I have been a very blessed person. I guess I've always known this; the trick is to know the blessings when you have them and not waste them.

For years now, whenever anyone would ask me, "How are you doing, Joe?" I would usually respond in one of two ways. Either;

"Every day is a new adventure,"

OR,

"I can't complain because no one would listen."

That second response is the one I mostly cling to. Because, even with all I've endured, I *still* know in my heart that ninety percent of the world would love to have my "problems".

I finally have God first and foremost in my life. I have an amazing wife, and together we have smart, healthy, strong kids who know right from wrong. I have friends I can count on, a home, food, and the ability to earn a good living.

Regrets nowadays are few. Although I do regret the harm I may have caused to people hurt along the way. But, all I can do is ask for their forgiveness.

I wouldn't change a thing. My past – and my mistakes – paved the way for what is now in my life and the man I have evolved into today.

As angry and disappointed as I am in my life choices and about what I've lost, I know it was me who made those choices. *No one else* ever forced me into them. Life is about the choices we make. At this point in my life, my current choice is to make a difference in the world.

I don't yet know how I'll do that, but this time around things will be different. In all the things I choose to do, and any differences that I may be blessed to make, I will do so knowing that I will perform only for an audience of *One*…

It's your life and you have your own choices to make, so make them carefully. What will you do? How will you make them? Whichever way you decide to go, you have but to remember one thing, this one key fact of life…

There are *no* grey areas.

About the Author:

Joseph N. Gagliano grew up on the northwest side of Chicago in a strong Italian-American family, the son of Chicago police officer and a housewife. Joe's family struggled to make ends meet until Joe was about thirteen years old, when the security company his father created grew to into a successful business.

He attended Eastern Illinois University, opened a few businesses and purchased several student rental properties. He dropped out of school early and began working on the trading floor of the Chicago Board of Trade in the bond futures trading pit.

As a young man on the trading floor of the CBOT, Joe's integrity was initially compromised. The trading environment was one of questionable ethics and seemed to embrace life's "grey areas". This learned acceptance tilted Joe's moral compass to a point that allowed him to rationalize many questionable opportunities for a period of time.

At age 24, Joe organized and financed the multi-million dollar, Arizona State basketball point shaving scandal in 1993-94. To this day, it remains one of the largest known scandals in sports history.

After being indicted for the ASU scandal, Joe lost his license to trade in the markets and was sentenced to federal prison. Struggling to get out from under the cloud of the ASU scandal, Joe went on to develop a chain of full service car washes that employed 500 plus employees. However, the ASU scandal continued to weigh on him personally and professionally.

Joe's run in's with the law were not yet over.

A few years later, the 2008 financial collapse engulfed the world and Joe's "grey area" in a banking deal landed him in jail for a 2nd term. Being labeled a 2-time felon led him down a dark path of depression and that nearly cost him his life.

It was also the wake up call he needed.

No Grey Areas is not just a story about right and wrong. It is Joe's personal story of greed, consequences and redemption. *No Grey Areas* is Joe's first book and a brutally honest telling of a slice of history, money, and family that will both captivate and inspire you.

Joe's new motto is simple, "Always perform for an Audience of One." Whether your "One" is faith based and driven by higher divine principles or the "One" is simply you. Performing for an "Audience of One" will hold you accountable for what is right and moral. All life choices - big or small - have an impact on our lives. If we can learn to keep our "Audience of One" happy, the rest of our stress will always fall into their proper places.

Joe is married and lives in Arizona with his wife and children.